NEW SWEDISH STYLE

New Swedish Style

Sasha Waddell

SPECIAL PHOTOGRAPHY BY PIA TRYDE

A PRACTICAL DECORATING GUIDE

Conran Octopus

To Ben and Atlanta

First published in 1996 by
Conran Octopus Limited
37 Shelton Street, London WC2H 9HN

Editorial Director: Suzannah Gough
Senior Editor: Jenna Jarman
Editorial Assistant: Helen Woodhall
Editors: Alison Bolus, Sarah Sears
Art Editor: Alison Fenton
Illustrator: Carolyn Jenkins
Picture Research: Claire Taylor
Production Controller: Jill Beed
Indexer: Indexing Specialists

British Library Cataloguing-in-Publication Data
A catalogue record for this book is available from the British Library.

ISBN 1 85029 842 4

Printed in Hong Kong

CONTENTS

INTRODUCTION

WAYS WITH WOOD

DECORATING WITH FABRIC

COLOUR AND PAINT

INTRODUCING THE LOOK

As a Scot, I share the Scandinavians' love of the clear northern light. It has a cool whiteness that can be dazzling to the eye and uplifting to the soul. One of the first principles of Swedish style is to bring this light into the home.

I first discovered Swedish style – and, in fact, Scandinavian style in general – when I was a drama student in the 1960s, through the plays of Ibsen and Strindberg. Sparsely furnished and yet still romantic, the sets reflected the Scandinavians' love of nature and their attempts to recreate it indoors. Then, in the mid-1970s, a theatre designer friend, who often designed ballet sets for the Theatre Royal in Stockholm, started to send me postcards; as well as photographs of Swedish interiors, there were illustrations by Carl Larsson, a painter-illustrator famous for his simple, elegant drawings and paintings of his family and home in Sundborn, Sweden, who worked at the turn of the twentieth century. It was really the interiors of Larsson's home that caught my imagination. It felt as if I had been searching for years for exactly that

'Learn the Swedish art of paring down and keeping things simple.'

unpretentious look, and that emphasis on light and simplicity. There was such clarity and yet it was so cosy.

When I started my career as an interior designer, Carl Larsson's drawings and illustrations continued to be uppermost in my mind as I rebelled against the opulence of 1980s fashion; indeed, I became completely obsessed with recreating the Swedish look. And at that stage I had not even visited Sweden. When I finally did cross the North Sea, it was the castles and manor houses that made the greatest impression on me. They were more formal and often much grander than Larsson's home, but that essentially Swedish simplicity was still evident.

Calm and light, unassuming and uncluttered, the Swedish look is not only attractive to the eye but easy to live with too. In my own design work, I have tried to use the spirit of authentic Swedish style as inspiration for designing my own interiors today; rather than slavishly copying all the individual elements, I interpret the original source. I hope that you too will be inspired.

This sitting room in central London encapsulates the key elements of Swedish design: simplicity, symmetry and the maximum use of light.

WHAT IS SWEDISH STYLE?

As a designer, I never cease to be fascinated by the visual connections between historical styles; and there are so many cross-references that there is always a huge fund from which to draw ideas. Finding myself sympathetically inclined towards Swedish style, I became especially interested to see how interior design had evolved in Scandinavia over the centuries.

In Sweden, in the mid-eighteenth century, the court architect Carl Hårleman imported French artists and craftsmen to work on the royal palaces, because the French court was the envy of the civilized world and thus was the model to which every other court aspired. As in most European countries in the eighteenth century, a cross-fertilization of styles occurred as a result of trade, royal marriages, and diplomatic visits by foreign ambassadors. And the lavish rococo exuberance that arrived from France was tempered in Sweden by a certain frugality which resulted in a charming simplicity.

'A home is not a lifeless object but a living entity, and like everything that is alive it must obey the law of nature.'
Carl Larsson

In the late eighteenth century Prince Gustav returned from the French court of Louis XVI to become King Gustav III of Sweden. He introduced a more restrained classical form to his royal palace, inspired by the new neo-classical style he had enjoyed in France during his stay there. The schemes were light in colour and touch, with tall windows, pier glass mirrors and pale wooden floors, and with chairs placed formally around the room. New, more efficient tiled stoves made it possible to open up suites of rooms, so the whole atmosphere became light and airy and acquired the clean, unpretentious look that has come to be associated today with Swedish style.

And then, at the beginning of the twentieth century, the eloquent style that characterized the castles and manor houses of nineteenth-century Sweden was updated and made more relevant for everyday life by Carl Larsson and his textile-designer wife Karin. His charming and elegant domestic paintings which

Pale grey, panelled walls, formally arranged furniture and a clear vista
all help to create a tranquil feel in an eighteenth-century dining room.

portrayed his own domestic life show how, if cleverly refined, the style could work equally well in more modest environments.

The extraordinary open-air museum at Skansen, in Stockholm, has buildings taken from all over Sweden. Manor houses, rural buildings, an artist's studio and an apothecary's shop, among others, have all been carefully renovated and furnished as they would have been originally to illustrate domestic and working life as it was in these places. It is possible to see here the combination of the grand and the humble that is so typically Swedish: elegant furniture positioned sparingly in airy rooms, combined with modest fabrics, timber panelling or pretty rococo swags painted on stretched panels of canvas on the walls.

Authentic Swedish style not only creates a tranquil atmosphere but a look that is inviting and romantic too. Light is essential in Swedish design, and natural light particularly, so curtains should let in as much light as possible. Unlined muslin curtains are the obvious choice, for they filter the light and, blowing gently in the breeze, they never fail to create a summery atmosphere – bringing the outside into the home. Walls in pale, receding colours enhance the feeling of space and calm, and light timber floors, with modest cotton runners, reflect the light. Typically, furniture is used sparingly and placed according to the formal French manner.

Painting furniture in off-whites or pale French greys keeps the look light and airy. One or two pieces of furniture painted just a couple of shades darker than the walls give a wonderfully ethereal

Above: The bedroom of the king's mistress in Gripsholm Castle is tiny. Yet it still includes a number of design features key to Swedish style: the walls are painted with delicate sprigs of flowers and berries; the basic bed frame is dressed with pale pink gingham that matches the bedspread as well as the chair seat cover. The little gilt mirror is typical too, lending a touch of opulence.

Opposite: The charm of this room at Skansen results from the way the naïve combines with the sophisticated. The tiny bed is completely out of scale in a room of these proportions but it is a delightful feature. Beside it is a plain, grey-painted Swedish version of an English ladder-back chair. Touches of colour on the bed drapes and on the wall lift the grey of the room.

Left: This room in Svindersvik epitomizes Swedish style. The extremely long, elegant sofa with turned legs, the tiled stove and the pale-washed floorboards could make it look rather cold, but the rose-red checked upholstery, the soft yellow ochre of the painted, panelled walls and the blue-and-white design of the tiles make it appear very inviting.

quality. And upholstering a traditional sofa with a loose cover of off-white linen will soften its formality. Mixing the grand with the humble is typically Swedish too; painted rustic furniture beneath a grand gilt mirror is a characteristically quirky but delightful visual mixture. Symmetry is another important ingredient of the Swedish look and I am always aware of this when placing furniture or objects in a room. Framing a window, for example, with two chairs is a simple device that lends a refined sense of balance and order.

If your imagination has been fired by the Swedish look, as mine was, and you want to recreate its essence, follow a few basic rules: keep it light and simple, and always pare down the unnecessary.

GETTING STARTED

Anyone who has had their home decorated knows the agonies of organizing builders, carpenters and plasterers, and the nightmare of getting furniture and fabrics delivered on time. As decisions often have to be made on the spot, it is essential to have thought through the fundamentals of what you have in mind for a room before the work starts. Even if you have to do the work yourself, you should be absolutely clear about your design plans.

You should decide first of all on the function of the room because there is no point in designing a room that looks beautiful, but which does not meet your practical needs. Equally, however, a room dedicated solely to its function with no regard to its look can be both very unwelcoming and uninspiring if it has not been visualized properly. Always maintain a balanced approach.

When you start to plan a room, you should measure everything – the architraves, the skirting and so on – and then you should take some photographs. These will give you a feel for the whole room. You then need to draw a floor plan, which you should make to scale on graph paper, or using a scale rule. (This is not as difficult as it sounds.) Looking at the plan, you must now try to visualize being in the room, and start to think about how you will treat the walls, what furniture will be suitable and where it will be placed. Remember that you have to think about whether particular areas of the room need to have different functions – for reading,

The strong, brightly checked walls are prevented from becoming overpowering by the restraint of the pale, painted panelling below. The humble style of the rustic green chest of drawers contrasts well with the more elaborate mirror and wall sconces, demonstrating how to successfully combine the simple and the grand.

'Interior design is like a game of chess – every move or decision you make will shape the end result.'

watching television, etc. – and define these areas in your mind. Above all, keep all your designs simple. It is easy to have ideas; the difficulty lies in resolving them well. The most wonderful ideas badly resolved can look dreadful; while on the contrary, the most ordinary can look fabulous, if sensitively executed.

When you have all your ideas on paper, talk them over with your builder or carpenter (or seek advice if you are doing it on your own) and discuss any practical problems your plans may present. Be prepared to go back to the drawing board in order to achieve a design that is of practical and aesthetic value.

To achieve a Swedish look you should consider the important ingredients of traditional Swedish style. Look at symmetry and how you can use it to best effect because it provides focal points for the room and brings to it a sense of order and calm. Panelling can create a dramatic symmetrical effect, as can the way furniture and decorative objects are arranged.

When you have done this, you will need to think about which fabrics you are going to use: muslins and cottons with checks, stripes and little flower sprigs are all typically Swedish. Collect a selection of fabric swatches and then think about colour and pattern, and you will find that certain fabrics just seem to 'fit'.

Once again at Svindersvik, ornate elements are combined with the plain to dramatic effect. A lavish clock hangs centrally above two eighteenth-century chairs upholstered in a simple checked fabric, placed on each side of an ornate walnut secretaire, but the pale, washed floorboards bring the the look down to earth.

COMBINING OLD AND NEW

To display expensive antique china alongside modern, inexpensive pieces can be very exciting and effective; I have always loved this combination. Focus attention on the best piece by positioning it centrally, and then build up your display symmetrically. A combination display like this usually works best if it is unified by colour, so an all green-and-white or an all blue-and-white collection will look spectacular. Two pieces might jar if their colours do not match exactly; but if you build up blue upon blue – three, four or five together – then they will start to complement each other. It is probably better to avoid large collections in one solid colour, however, which might look heavy.

Hard-glazed pieces – china or tiles – can bring a delicate feel to a room, the fired glaze making the colours and designs pretty but not sentimental. And while it would be impractically expensive to install a traditional Swedish tiled stove today, it is still possible to recreate something of the original decorative effect with modern tiles. New Mexican and reproduction Delft tiles are good substitutes for authentic designs in the alcoves of fireplaces.

It is relatively easy, too, to buy an old, unpromising-looking piece of furniture and introduce it into a scheme as long as its shape and proportions are good. Painted all one colour and subtly aged, and mixed with new pieces painted in the same way, it will work well, and become an integral part of an ordered design.

Opposite: When I designed this London dining room, antique accessories were combined strategically with a dining table and chairs from my own furniture collection: the Edwardian reproduction of a French rococo clock, for instance, sits happily on the newly designed mantelshelf.

Right: The display on these shelves perfectly illustrates how it is possible to combine pieces from different periods. I have mixed modern, department-store china with antique family pieces, and a strongly coloured, light-hearted 1920s tea set. The off-white woodwork acts as a frame for this three-dimensional picture.

I have bought a hideous mock-Louis XV piece and transformed it by replacing the handles and painting it a soft greeny-beige. I also sometimes use a reproduction chandelier, but paint it off-white and trail ivy over it. Somehow the ivy 'ages' the look of a new chandelier, which may not be as delicate as an original.

'Do not be afraid to introduce your favourite old pieces of furniture, china or fabric.'

DISPLAY AND FINISHING TOUCHES

In the context of Swedish-style design, finishing touches should be subtle, characterized by a degree of restraint and determined by an eye for detail. A well-planned and ordered interior can be completely ruined if too many diverse objects are introduced, so stand back and take a look every time you hang a picture or place an object: each item needs to work within the overall scheme.

Pictures are an all-important part of the design of a room, but must be hung properly to be effective. People often hang them too high when in fact they look far better at eye level – or even lower. Using ribbons to hang small pictures is both simple and looks Swedish, but keep the bows small and neat, as floppy bows can look sentimental. Obviously, good oil paintings are expensive, but I sometimes put postcards of portraits in small oval frames to very good effect, and black-and-white engravings can look wonderful too – especially in a pale-painted room. For the best effect either use dark frames or paint them the same colour as the walls.

I often display plates decoratively on the wall and find this is an inexpensive and useful way of finalizing the Swedish look of a room. They are particularly effective if arranged symmetrically. Alternatively, use shelves or racks to house more of your china: if you can, display entire sets, but otherwise try a mixture of your favourites, making sure that different shapes, patterns and sizes are arranged symmetrically, with large plates or a jug in the middle, and identically sized plates on each side. As the pairs of items increase in number, so the arrangement's effect becomes more dramatic. But remember the importance of restraint: nothing is so quintessentially Swedish as a simple plate rack filled exclusively with pewter plates – though this is obviously quite costly.

Otherwise you can create a 'tablescape' very simply with a few beautiful objects: a cream china tureen, for instance, filled with

'Before homing in on detail, always stand back and look at the room as a whole.'

Above: A delightful little lithograph by Carl Larsson of his daughter Lisbeth is set in a reeded frame painted off-white to match the walls. The antique cream ribbon with pale brown edging, tied in a simple bow, could perhaps have come from Carl Larsson's own parlour.

Opposite: Blue and white is always a successful combination and when carried to extremes it can create a stunning effect, as the kitchen in Skogaholm Manor demonstrates. Stacking an entire dinner service into a traditional plate rack creates a simple, yet dramatic focal point.

flowers, and flanked by candlesticks – either made of pewter or painted the same colour as the walls. And crisply ironed antique table runners with simple embroidery or drawn-thread work not only break up a large expanse of table but – with a vase of wild flowers upon them – will lend any room a charming, homely feel.

Whatever finishing touches you add, keep everything simple and symmetrical, and you will not go far wrong.

Above: This room in Carl Larsson's own house illustrates the Swedish obsession for bringing the outside into their homes. Ranks of geraniums stand in pots along the window sill and ivy trails delicately across the top of the window to achieve this effect.

LIGHT AND LIGHTING

The image of pale light filtering through muslin curtains and falling delicately on a vase of flowers is, for me, typically Swedish. And certainly everything about Swedish interior design seems to focus on bringing that special light into the home, or augmenting it in the most sympathetic, least intrusive way. The people of Sweden, like all Scandinavians, are passionately obsessive about daylight, primarily because their winters are so long and dark.

Blond, natural woods and pale-coloured walls, floors, furniture and fabrics are all enhanced by the effects created by natural light. You can use mirrors too in all sorts of ways to produce dramatic lighting effects; positioned carefully, they can reflect the light from outside, which can even magnify the apparent size of a room. And this airy, spacious look will be further emphasized by uncluttered, simple furnishing.

Undoubtedly, when not soaked in natural daylight, rooms always look best by candlelight. Traditionally, and typically – even

Left: Candlelight is always very atmospheric; it is a soft and softening light. The warm glow given to the off-white walls by the candlelight in this hallway in Skansen produces a wonderful, ethereal quality.

Opposite: I wanted this south-facing London room to capture the atmosphere of a Swedish summer house, with the French windows thrown open behind the cream roller blind trimmed with antique lace, the white muslin curtains billowing in the breeze, and sunlight falling brightly onto a vase of flowers.

now – the long, dark, Arctic winter nights are lit by candles that bring warmth and intimacy to the home. Candelabras can create an elegant atmosphere, and more than enough light by which to eat. I once lit a very large pair of Swedish candelabras, each bearing twenty-two candles and not only did they cast a wonderfully mellow light, they also gave off immense heat.

Obviously, it is not always possible to use only candlelight. And in order to capture something of the same feel with electric light, you must choose your lamp bases and shades with great care. Whatever style you choose, it is vital to balance the proportions of the shade and base, as nothing looks worse than a small base with a heavy shade, or vice versa. If you want a large lamp, a blue-and-white Chinese pot with a pleated cream silk shade can be very successful, as can a candlestick-style base painted off-white (or in a similarly pale colour) with a simple shade of parchment, checked or pleated cotton, or cream silk again. Even an electric light will give out a very soft, attractive light if the cream silk shade is lined with a silk of the palest pink.

A chandelier can be very beautiful and elegant if you choose well: if it is too small, it may look like an apology, and if it is too large, it may overpower the room. The bare bulbs can also give a very harsh light unless controlled by a dimmer. Small, frosted bulbs are best (usually made in France), being infinitely preferable to the more common large bulbs, which tend to detract attention from the delicacy of the chandelier itself.

'Bringing natural light indoors is the key to Swedish design and to my interiors.'

CHAPTER ONE

WAYS WITH WOOD

The dining room in Carl Larsson's house in Sundborn shows quite clearly how his designs were closely related to those of the English Arts and Crafts Movement – an influential force in the European design world at the turn of the century.

I have taken much inspiration from this room, updating the very 'period' atmosphere – the dark panelling, leather squabs, the painted wall decoration and the shapes of the motifs – by using instead pale, receding colours to create a fresher, prettier look.

WOOD IN INTERIORS

Wood plays an all-important role in Swedish domestic architecture. Employed extensively inside the house, it also has a long and strong tradition in all the Baltic countries as a basic building material. Beech, birch and pine are the most popular woods, Swedish pine being paler and more silvery than other pines. Hardwoods are rarely used: the only mahogany-panelled room I have ever seen in Sweden was built by a Scottish family.

Inside the house, one is at once keenly aware of the presence of natural timber, not least because, typically, the large, uncluttered expanse of floor in any room is of pale wood. And, of course, the panelling, mouldings and furniture are made of wood too, though these are often decoratively painted. The contrast between this sophistication and the rustic quality of the natural floorboards creates a charming and essentially Swedish look.

Carl Larsson often used wooden panelling – in his own idiosyncratic way – and it is still an extremely popular form of wall covering. Typically, walls are clad in vertical tongue-and-groove panelling which reaches three-quarters of the way up the wall. This is then finished off with a shelf, supported by simple decorative cut-out brackets. Not only does this look delightful, it is also extremely functional. Indeed, I have often extended the tongue-and-groove right up to the top of the door frame, and then fitted a shelf above it that runs the whole way round the room.

'Keep things simple: the most wonderful ideas badly resolved look dreadful; the most ordinary ones sensitively resolved can look fabulous.'

Wooden mouldings are another distinctive feature of Swedish style that differ from their French and English counterparts. Skirtings are very plain, architraves always simple, and dado rails are not only much flatter but are often so low that they might almost be termed a high skirting. I often use a door architrave instead of a traditional dado rail because its flatter shape and cleaner lines are more in keeping with the look of traditional Swedish mouldings.

The thing that I find delightful about Sweden is the abundance of original visual reference material available. Because that dreadful habit of knocking down interior walls does not exist over there, original skirtings and cornices are still in place, and rooms retain their original proportions and sense of scale.

If you think laterally when you look at original Swedish woodwork, your imagination will undoubtedly be fired. Porches over front doors can inspire interior cupboards or alcoves; a rustic casing for a kitchen towel rail can be transformed into a curtain pelmet or decorative light pelmet (see page 35). But always remember that having the idea is the easy part; the job of getting the proportions right, making sure the idea works, and ensuring that it is not overdone is much more difficult.

The bedroom in the Tottie's house in the Skansen open-air museum is a good example of how to use simple mouldings; the dado rail here is almost flat. This very simple style of moulding is now quite difficult – sometimes impossible – to find. It may be that you will have to custom-make your own design, by building up different layers of mouldings. It is also possible to create fielded panels (panels with a plain raised central area) using this layering method.

This staircase, backstage at the Drottningholm Court Theatre, inspired my own balustraded radiator covers. The exaggerated curves of the flat, cut-out shapes create an effective illusion. And the shape of the space between each column is as important as the column itself; it is the interaction of the two shapes which creates the effect. Such two-dimensional balustrades are widespread in Sweden – on staircases, verandas and as decorative reliefs.

PANELLING

Even if a room is well-proportioned, it can still be made to appear larger and grander by using formal panelling. The trick is to keep the dado rail low, which makes the walls appear higher. There is an infinite number of sizes and arrangements of panelling, but whatever you choose, it will have the effect of introducing symmetry and order into a room.

Before you start to design the panelling, look at as much visual reference material as you can – in other people's houses and in books – in order to understand the logic of the panelling in particular rooms, because no two rooms are resolved in the same way. As a general rule, however, the largest wall will usually have a wide central panel flanked by two narrower ones, and a shorter wall will often be divided into three panels of equal widths.

My method of panelling is very simple and not too expensive. I fix strips of medium-density fibreboard (MDF) directly onto the wall to act as the panel frames and then the areas of wall between them become the centres of the panels. Once the frames and walls have been painted the same colour, the effect is wonderful.

A room panelled in tongue-and-groove will have quite a different atmosphere from one with more formal panelling. Tongue-and-groove is made up of planks of timber, each with a tongue on one edge and a groove on the other edge, which are locked tightly into each other. Although it looks easy to fit, there

'When judging proportions only your eye knows what is right.'

are many design decisions that must be made before the panelling is fixed – whether you are doing it yourself or using a carpenter – decisions which are the key to a well-designed room. Spending longer at the thinking stage will certainly cost you less in time and money than rushing these decisions. And it is worth remembering that because tongue-and-groove is fixed in place by battens, and these battens can be of varying depths to provide an even surface, the cladding can be used to cover up huge problem areas. Do be careful, however, that the total depth of the battens and panelling is not so great that it stands proud of any architraves and skirtings already in place, which would then have to be removed. If in doubt, talk to a carpenter.

I generally use tongue-and-groove in bathrooms and kitchens; not only for its insulation qualities but also because it produces a cosy yet chic look. Equally, however, it can have a marvellous effect in a sitting room: painted French grey and extending from floor to ceiling, for example, with architraves and skirtings in off-white, and with a large, ornate mirror, it combines the modest and sophisticated with typical Scandinavian flair.

There is a variety of tongue-and-groove panelling styles from which to choose, but whichever you pick, remember to keep your design plain and simple for the best possible effect.

Above: Here is a detail of the panelling, at the corner of a window recess. Once it has been painted, and a curtain hung, it is difficult to identify the centre of the panel as being only of plaster and the panel frames as being of humble MDF.

Left: I used an architrave instead of a traditional dado rail when I designed this panelled room because I wanted a flatter effect. The panelling is actually strips of MDF attached to the walls. Painting the whole surface in one colour completes the look.

A shelf above a scrubbed beech worktop, supported by decorative cut-out brackets. Set against a background of white-painted tongue-and-groove panelled walls, it is both attractive and a practical feature in a country-style kitchen.

A selection of samples and templates for cut-outs in my studio, to be used for pelmets, decorative brackets, cornices, shelf fronts, cabinet tops and radiator covers. All these shapes were inspired by the abundant woodwork I found in eighteenth- and nineteenth-century houses all over Sweden.

DECORATIVE CUT-OUT SHAPES

Wherever you look in Sweden – on doorways, verandas, staircases and furniture – there are French rococo curves, baroque carvings, classical Greek mouldings and Islamic forms, but all simplified to a simple wooden silhouette. If these shapes seem familiar, it is probably because you have noticed something similar on the canopies of English railway stations, on the bases of French provincial furniture, in Turkish wall niches, on rustic American furniture, or somewhere else equally unlikely. A visual pattern book seems to exist that is totally universal, and used with imagination and flair, these flat shapes can make pretty, decorative additions to entire schemes and individual pieces alike. Most three-dimensional shapes can be represented in silhouette so there is lots of scope for bursts of imagination.

I often use wooden cut-outs in my interior and furniture designs because they add wit and charm to any room. I have, for instance, designed decorative cut-out brackets as supports for semi-circular shelves displaying plates and ornaments. This type of bracket can also be particularly attractive on a shelf just above a kitchen work surface, especially if the walls are clad with tongue-and-groove. Alternatively, a decorative cut-out edging along the front of the shelf can hide any ugly battens (see page 30). Equally, a cut-out pelmet can transform a window, simultaneously hiding unattractive tracks, or the trappings of roller blinds, and giving a simple, yet decorative frame to the curtains when in use.

'Choose simple shapes that you are familiar with as these make the most successful designs.'

DECORATIVE SHELF EDGING

Shelves are as much for show and display as for storage and can look very insubstantial and unprepossessing if left with naked edges, especially if these are badly painted. Most shelves can, however, be easily rescued through the addition of some simple decorative edgings.

These are made on the basis of a template, which in practice is little different from a sewing pattern; it serves as a guide to where the wood is to be cut, just as a pattern determines the shape into which fabric is cut.

You don't need to be a great draughtsman to make a successful template. It is really a matter of using basic shapes to advantage. Most people find drawing templates full-size far easier than drawing small designs. Start by looking at shapes, drawing shapes, photographing and copying shapes; soon you will be able to rough out an idea for a decorative edging, and if you relax, you may even find that as well as the head telling the hand what to draw, the hand will just start to take over.

Even if you have no experience of carpentry, this project is still for you, as you will be able to design exactly what you want and then have it made up by a carpenter. Once you have mastered these shelf edgings you could make templates for all sorts of decorative cut-outs (see the decorative light pelmet and day bed projects on pages 35 and 38).

Opposite: Decorative cut-out shelf edgings look pretty, and also hide the supporting battens. Blue-and-white accessories on a blue-painted shelf accentuate the effect.

Above: I designed this tiny pale blue-and-white bedroom with a built-in bed to form a sofa. I put the desk, with shelves above it, in an alcove to maximize space.

TEMPLATE FOR DECORATIVE SHELF EDGINGS : PROJECT

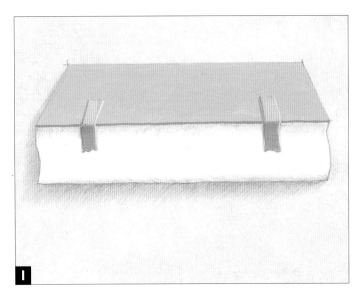

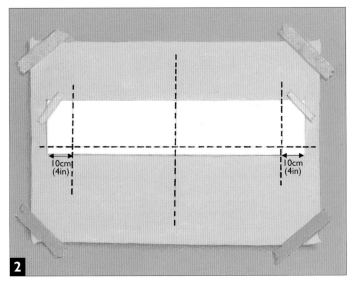

YOU WILL NEED:
MATERIALS
Sheet of 12mm (½in) MDF or
substitute material • Wood glue •
Panel pins (nails) • Acrylic
primer • Wood filler • Eggshell
paint • Flat oil paint

TOOLS AND EQUIPMENT
Large sheet of plain paper •
Tape measure • Soft pencil •
Scissors • Masking tape •
Tracing paper • Set square
(triangle) • Ruler • Plates of
various sizes • Large sheets of
cardboard • Jigsaw • Hammer •
Nail punch • Fine sandpaper •
25mm (1in) paintbrush

1 Cut out a piece of paper
to the measured length of
the shelf by approx. 12.5cm
(5in) deep. Lightly tape it to
the edge of the shelf and
fold it under to test what
depth of edging looks best;
don't make it so deep that
you restrict the space below.
Mark the desired depth in
pencil and cut off the excess
paper. Take the paper off the
shelf, tape a larger piece of
tracing paper over it and
trace off its dimensions.

2 Using a set square
(triangle), draw a line
down the tracing paper to
mark the centre of the template; your design must be
symmetrical to the left and
right of this line. Now at the
bottom of the template, measure in from both sides to
create a width of 'frame'
within which the decorative
shapes will be cut. This
frame needs to be wide
enough not only to cover the
side struts and any side fixings but also to balance the
cut-out design. (In this project 10cm[4in] was allowed

at either side, but you could
easily make it less.) Now
draw a dotted horizontal line
2.5cm (1in) up from the bottom edge to act as a guide-
line for the design.

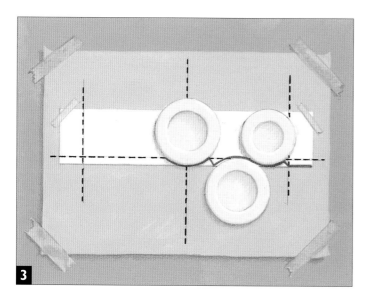

3

4

3 Drawing round the rims of plates offers a quick means of establishing gentle, regular curves, so gather a selection of dinner and soup plates for this purpose. Design one side of the shelf only, because you will later trace the mirror image of what you design on to the other side. Centre the first plate on the central line of the shelf and then work to one side from this point, pushing the edges of the plates from above and below into the area between the bottom line and the dotted guide line, some close together and others spaced a little apart. Draw round their edges within this area to establish a sequence of concave and convex curves. Join any spaces between the curves with straight lines or freehand curves so as to create a single, meandering but controlled line that reaches from the centre of the shelf to the outer horizontal 'frame' line. Trace off the mirror image of this line on to the other side of the paper. A decorative cut-out shape is now established; if you are not quite satisfied with it, repeat the exercise or else overlay another piece of tracing paper and trace the design off with modifications. You can, of course, choose a different design from the one shown here.

4 Trace the finished design onto cardboard, cut round the entire shelf edging shape and hold this 'dummy' up against the shelf to check that it fits and the proportions work. Adjust if necessary. Draw around the shape onto the MDF. Cut out the MDF with a jigsaw and fix to the shelf with wood glue and panel pins (nails), punched well in with a nail punch. Prime, fill and sand down the decorative front and then paint with one or two coats of eggshell and a final coat of flat oil paint.

MOULDINGS

Mouldings are lengths of wood used simply to hide junctions and joins in a decorative way. Architrave mouldings can hide the junction between the plaster wall and the timber door- or window-frame, while decorative mouldings can be used to hide the hairline gaps between a fitted cupboard and the wall of an alcove. Panel and astragal mouldings decorate the walls of a room or the face of a door, and dado rails run around the room at chair height. Cornices for the tops of cabinets and bookshelves can be made of mouldings, and they can also be used to dress up a secondhand piece of furniture. They offer the quickest and most effective means of transforming a room or cabinet.

Mouldings used in Swedish interiors are usually plain and simple. So when you look for mouldings yourself, choose plain, well-proportioned ones. Remember also that once they are in place the mouldings will appear much smaller than when you see them out of context, especially if they are placed high above eye level. It is difficult to choose mouldings from catalogue drawings and, unless you are really experienced, impossible to tell from these what they will look like when applied. Most people tend to use mouldings that are far too small and which look insignificant and uncomfortable. Bear this in mind when you try out sample pieces and choose those that are large enough. Before you start, look at as much visual reference as you can: observe mouldings in

Left: This pretty blue wardrobe is from my Linnaeus Collection. A simple architrave acts as a cornice and the shape is emphasized by an additional flat top. The mouldings create a decorative yet deliberately simple relief.

Opposite: Sample lengths of mouldings are an invaluable tool to help you imagine the final design; it is hard to get a real feel from a drawing in a catalogue.

'Mouldings should be used to enhance a room's character and should not shout out for attention.'

rooms, on pieces of furniture – and in this book. Ask yourself why it doesn't look good; how it could have looked better; if it is the size, shape or placement that makes it work particularly well.

Ask at the hardware store for some spare pieces that you can try out *in situ*. Narrow down your choice to two or three and buy some longer samples that can be mitred to give you a better impression of the finished effect. Finally, but importantly, remember that the stated dimensions are for unplaned mouldings and that you will lose about 3mm (⅛in) when 'finished'.

LIGHT PELMET

It is always a problem to find bathroom lighting suitable for Swedish-style interiors because the majority of lighting fixtures are art deco or neo-Victorian. I therefore decided to adapt the design of an antique Swedish kitchen towel rail, the roller of which was masked by a decorative pelmet.

As with the project for a decorative shelf edging, this project involves a cut-out shape that has the simple forms of country peasant style. I have kept the design painted upon it very basic so as not to detract from the shape of the wood; it consists simply of an upright diamond flanked by two diamonds lying on their sides, framed by a bordering outline. The painting need not be absolutely geometrically accurate; some irregularity tends to give a more unaffected and charming look.

If your light fitting is to be placed over a mirror, ensure that the proportions of the pelmet are in keeping with it. Think also about how high above the mirror the pelmet will have to be placed; as it will be above eye level, the decorative front must be deep enough to mask the light fitting beneath.

It is essential that the light fitting you choose is suitable for bathroom use and that you check with your electrical supplier or electrician the appropriate wattage and how much ventilation and clearance are required at the top and sides. If you don't take these factors into account the pelmet could become a fire risk.

Opposite: An unassuming yet decorative light pelmet hides the bathroom light fitting, its curves contrasting with the tongue-and-groove's strong vertical emphasis.

Above: Simple pale blue-and-white checked curtains, combined with hard-edged cladding on the walls, make a very pretty – but never sentimental – bathroom.

DECORATIVE LIGHT PELMET : PROJECT

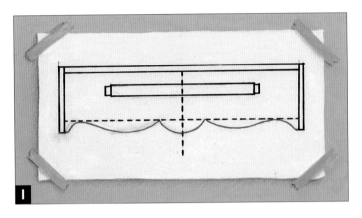

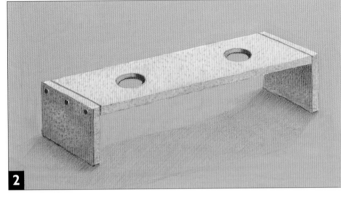

YOU WILL NEED:
MATERIALS
Light fitting • Sheet of 12mm (½in) MDF or substitute material • Wood glue • 2.5cm (1in) panel pins (nails) • Length of moulding • Acrylic primer • Wood filler • Matt vinyl emulsion (latex) • Artist's acrylic paint • Antiquing wax

TOOLS AND EQUIPMENT
Tape measure • Paper • Pencil • Cardboard • Panel saw • Drill • 5cm (2in) drill bit • Hammer • Nail punch • Masking tape • Jigsaw • Mitre block • Tenon saw • Fine sandpaper • 2.5cm (1in) paintbrush • Tracing paper • Nylon watercolour brush • Lint-free rag • Mirror plates (flush mounts)• Wall plugs (mollies) • Screws

1 Measure the width and height of the light fitting. Draw up these dimensions on paper and measure out from each side to the desired width of the pelmet, taking into account the required clearance (see below) and the width of the MDF side panels. Now mark in the clearance above the fitting advised by your electrical shop or electrician, plus the thickness of the MDF top. Measure down from the base of the fitting to the required depth of the pelmet – the lowest point of the cut-out shape – and very lightly draw a horizontal line to represent this, also marking in a dotted horizontal line approx. 4cm (1½in) above this to indicate the highest point of the cut-out shape. Now draw a short line of at least 2cm (¾in) in from each side at the bottom; the decorative shape should be designed within these framing margins. Now design a template for the front panel (see decorative shelf edging, page 29); this should cover the width and height of the pelmet (including the thickness of the side and top panels).

2 Using a panel saw, cut to size a piece of MDF for the top of the pelmet: this should be to the width of the template less twice the width of the MDF used for the side panels, and to the depth of the light fitting plus any advised clearance. Drill two large ventilation holes in this top of approx. 5cm (2in) in diameter. Cut the side pieces to the same depth as the top and the same height as the template. Now glue these pieces to the top, making sure that all edges align, and pin them using a hammer then a nail punch to drive the panel pins (nails) below the surface of the MDF for a neat finish.

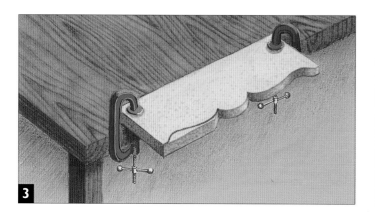

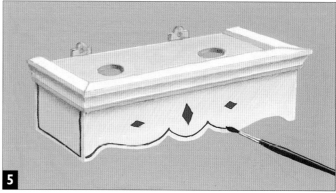

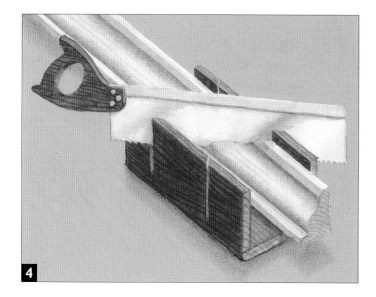

4 Choose a piece of moulding of suitable size for the top of the pelmet. Cut three lengths for the front and sides and mitre the corners with a tenon saw in a mitre block. Glue and pin the moulding to the front edge and then to the side edges. When the glue has dried, sand off uneven edges and, using the 2.5cm (1in) paintbrush, paint the pelmet with acrylic primer. Sand and fill the pin holes and the mitred corners. Sand again and paint with two coats of matt vinyl emulsion (latex) in your desired colour.

5 Design the painted decorative motif by sketching it on the cardboard template, then trace it off and lightly transfer the tracing to the painted front of the pelmet. Use artist's acrylic paint and a nylon watercolour brush to paint the diamond shapes and border line. Pencil in the border line on the sides, then go over it in acrylic. Finally, wax the pelmet with antiquing wax (see antiquing a table, page 93).

Attach two mirror plates (flush mounts) to the back of the pelmet and screw to the wall (drilling holes and inserting wall plugs [mollies] first), being careful to avoid electrical wires.

3 Lay the template over the front to check that it fits, then tape it to a piece of MDF, draw around it with a soft pencil and jigsaw out the shape. You will need to clamp the MDF to your workbench or table to keep it steady while you jigsaw it. Glue the resulting MDF cut-out panel to the front and pin as before.

SWEDISH DAY BED

This is an adapted copy of a Swedish day bed, adapted because the originals tend to be too narrow, uncomfortable to sleep in and complicated to make. The most commonly used form of convertable bed, the modern sofabed, can be cumbersome to fold in and out, and is also expensive. One alternative, if only a single bed is required in a room such as a study or a spare bedroom, is simply to put bolsters and cushions along the back and sides of an ordinary bed. The disadvantage of this is that they tend to fall off, and this is where the design of the Swedish day bed is so useful.

The day bed in this project is essentially a standard single divan with decorative wooden panels securely fixed around the back and sides to serve both as back- and armrests when it is used as a sofa and, if the arms are high enough, as head- and footboards when it is used as a bed. If the pillows have checked pillow slips that complement the bedspread they can serve equally well as cushions for the sofa. This may be a short cut which means that you don't have to spend ages making up the bed to look like a sofa, and vice versa, but it also looks extremely chic.

Whatever your design, ensure that your decorative wooden surround has no sharp edges and will be comfortable for both uses. For this project the surround and the decorative carving have been painted the same colour as the walls to achieve a simple look. To simplify it further you could leave out the carving.

A hand-carved wooden bow on the back of this Swedish-style day bed adds a delicate finishing touch to the otherwise very simple piece and sits well amidst formally placed cushions beneath white muslin curtains to create a very romantic look. Complementary colours – green and red – are combined here to marvellous effect.

SWEDISH DAY BED : PROJECT

YOU WILL NEED:
MATERIALS

Single divan with casters removed • 5 x 5cm (2 x 2in) batten lengths – two of bed length less 15cm (6in) and four of bed width less 15cm (6in); in all batten lengths, drill and countersink holes 30cm (12in) apart • 7.5cm (3in) screws • 4cm (1½in) screws • Large sheets of 20mm (¾in) thick MDF or substitute material • Wood glue • Carving (optional) • Panel pins (nails) • Primer • Wood filler • Eggshell paint • Flat oil paint

TOOLS AND EQUIPMENT

Tape measure • Pencil • Panel saw • Drill • Drill bits to suit gauge of screws • Screwdriver • Large sheets of cardboard • Masking tape • Scissors or craft knife • Jigsaw • Hammer • Nail punch • Fine sandpaper • 5cm (2in) paintbrush
NB You will lose approx. 3mm (⅛in) on 'finished' (prepared or planed) timber. You will need to take this into account when measuring up in step 2.

1 Measure and cut the required batten lengths (see left). Locate the top and bottom timber battens of the divan frame, and screw the drilled battens to them, leaving 7.5cm (3in) free at each side. These battens will provide sufficient clearance to allow bedclothes be tucked in around the mattress.

2 To calculate your working lengths, add 10cm (4in) to the length of your divan (5cm [2in] to each end to accommodate the battens), and add 12cm (4¾in) to the width of your divan (5cm [2in] for the back batten, 2cm [¾in] for the thickness of the back and 5cm [2in] for bedclothes at the front). Also measure the height of the divan, including the mattress.

3 Decide upon the height of the arms and back, remembering that the central decorative cut-out shape will be taller. (The bed surround

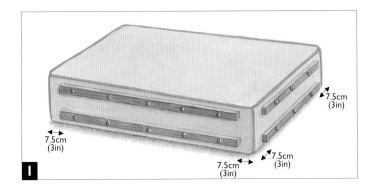

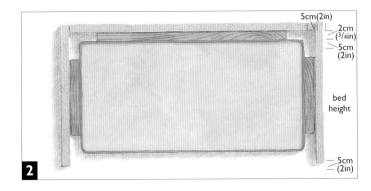

in this project is 79cm [31in] high, plus 9cm [3½in] for the cut-out shape.) Using your measurements, make templates in cardboard for the central cut-out shape and the top of the arms (see decorative shelf edging, page 29). Tape the back template to sheets of cardboard cut to the size of the complete back in order to judge its effect. Now do the same for one arm.

4 With a panel saw cut three large rectangles of MDF (or substitute material) for the back and sides, remembering to allow for the height of the cut-out on the back. Mark the centre of the back in pencil, tape your template to the MDF and draw around it, then repeat with the template for the side arms. Cut out the resulting shapes with a jigsaw.

5 Measure the position of the battens attached to the bed base and relay these to the MDF back and arms. Drill and countersink screw holes in the MDF to align with these battens. Join the back and arms with glue and screws, making sure that the corners are flush and true. Screw the back, then the side sheets of MDF to the bed frame.

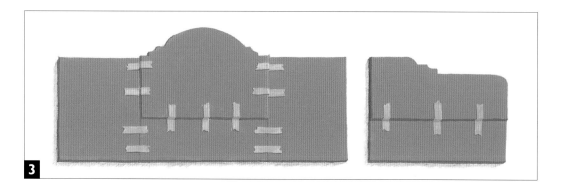

6 Position the carving (if you are using one) in the centre of the decorative cut-out area on the back, glue it on and fix it with panel pins (nails), using a nail punch to drive the pins below the surface of the wood. Now sand down any rough edges on the surround and paint with primer. Fill all holes and sand again. Paint with one coat of eggshell paint, leave to dry for 24 hours and sand again, then paint with one coat of flat oil paint of the same colour as the eggshell.

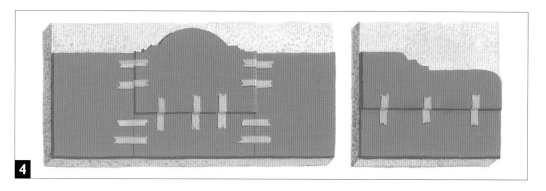

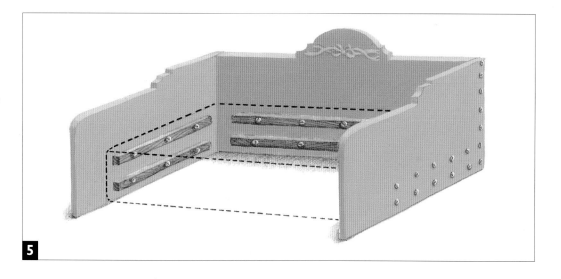

This radiator cover was inspired by a Swedish rural washstand and stands up as a piece of furniture in its own right. It serves as a heated place for folded towels, as an alternative to a hanging towel rail. The slatted door opens with a simple wooden latch and inside there is room to hang a small amount of washing. It is painted in off-white matt emulsion and waxed (see page 93).

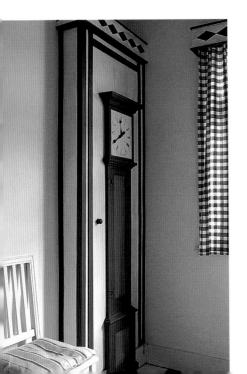

The secret behind the grandfather clock came from an idea inspired by rural Swedish beds, which were often built into the wall, almost forming a small room with built-in cupboards and sometimes a clock. I had the chance to make use of this idea in a bedroom for a little girl who wanted to disappear into the cupboard, as the children did in C.S. Lewis's The Lion, the Witch and the Wardrobe.

DISGUISING UNWANTED FEATURES

Some modern fixtures and appliances, such as radiators, sound systems and televisions, are undeniably unattractive, but nonetheless they are part of everyday life today. And so a little bit of lateral thinking is required to find a solution to the two major design problems they present: where to put them and how to make them less incongruous whilst allowing them to function efficiently. Generally speaking, though, use a light touch and a bit of wit and it will be easy.

Radiators are ugly but essential in a modern centrally heated home, and a good cover, while screening the radiator from view, should obviously allow as much heat convection as possible. So I never box in my radiators but leave them open at the sides and design large-scale decorative panels for the front, cutting patterns out of them to allow as much heat as possible to escape, yet leaving the valves and controls readily accessible and making the covers very easy to fit. A shelf above a cover distracts the eye from the radiator and also provides additional display or storage space.

Various things have inspired my designs for these radiator screens: a staircase at the Theatre Royal, Drottningholm, gave me the idea for a flat cut-out balustrade design, and Carl Larsson's fence prompted my garden gate design (see page 45), while an old washstand inspired the open-slatted wooden unit I built around a radiator in a bathroom.

'The best ideas are witty ones that come from lateral thinking and have a light touch.'

In a panelled room, of course, the rhythm of the panelling can be accentuated by creating a repetitive pattern with a rhythm of its own on the front of the radiator cover. If you are designing a panelled room from scratch, it is important to use radiators that stand below the height of the dado rail so that the dado rail can merely be extended to run around the front of the cover; the top of the cover thus aligns with the dado rail, making the cover an integral part of the panelling.

Sound systems with big speakers are another abhorrent modern appliance. Whenever I can, I like to put them into alcoves where they may be screened like radiators, with decorative cut-out or slatted doors that will allow the sound to escape.

And then, of course, there is nearly always a television which needs to be hidden. I have often bought an old cabinet to house a television and doctored it to suit a room, but I have also designed cabinets from scratch, based on French linen presses, and these are the most successful.

Sometimes it is diverting to disguise a perfectly acceptable feature just for the sheer fun of it. Children's rooms in particular are full of brilliant opportunities, and it is wonderful to see what original ideas your children dream up if you get them to join in right at the very beginning of the planning stage.

Covering up unused fireplaces can be difficult. Firescreens can take up too much room and a solid panel blocking the area is decidedly unattractive. So, using some simple cut-out shapes – to give a feeling of depth – and surrounding the panel with hand-painted Mexican tiles reminiscent of Old Delft (often used by the Swedes), I created an authentic Swedish look to solve a largely modern problem.

Inspired by a staircase at the Court Theatre in Drottningholm (see page 23), this simple flat cut-out balustrade not only hides the radiator, it is a decorative feature in itself. Make the shelf the height of a console table, and you will have a display area too. Hang a mirror above the shelf and the proportions of the effect will be lent a certain elegance, then paint the cover white in contrast with greeny-grey walls for freshness.

43

GARDEN GATE RADIATOR COVER

This cover was directly inspired by the fence and gate outside Carl Larsson's house in Sundborn, Sweden, which suggested to me the idea that a radiator cover could not only look like a gate, but could also function like one.

The more simply constructed the cover, the easier it is to use. I avoided creating a bulky structure with complicated panels that had to be removed in favour of a wittier and more practical design: simple, hinged 'gates', like cupboard doors, can be opened quickly to give full and easy access to the controls and valves.

The cover in this example has been designed for a radiator in an alcove, although it could have sides if need be. Even if your radiator is low, the gate doors make a good base for a shelf, so taking into account the overall proportions of the alcove, adjust the height of the cover accordingly. Check too that the alcove is deep enough for the cover to give the radiator at least a 4cm (1½in) clearance.

The beauty of the garden gate design is that it can be simply constructed from wooden battens and offers excellent heat convection. It is, however, just one of an infinite number of designs. With just a little more skill you could create a template (see the decorative shelf edging or light pelmet projects, pages 29 and 35) for decorative cut-out doors or a single cut-out flat frontage made of MDF (or substitute material).

Opposite: It is very important to maintain the balance of a wall once you have disguised the radiator. Here I have created a dresser effect with decorative shelves; painted off-white and set against yellow-ochre walls they make the perfect setting for this Royal Doulton dinner service.

Above: References to Carl Larsson's home are scattered throughout this sunny, yellow-ochre dining room; the shelves were inspired by brackets in his dining room; the radiator cover design was sparked off by his garden fence; and the slatted-back chair and the long antique table runner frequently feature in illustrations of his home.

GARDEN GATE RADIATOR COVER : PROJECT

YOU WILL NEED:

MATERIALS

Prepared battens (as detailed in steps) • Sheet of 2cm (¾in) MDF (or substitute material) • Screws (8 or 10 gauge) • Wood glue • 2.5cm (1in) panel pins (nails) • Four brass butt hinges • Wood filler • Acrylic primer • Paint • Brass hook and eye fitting

TOOLS AND EQUIPMENT

Tape measure • Pencil • Straight edge • Tenon saw • Spirit level • Hammer • Drill • Drill bits to suit gauges of screws, plus countersink bit • Jigsaw • Wall plugs (mollies) • Screwdriver • Panel saw • Nail punch • Chisel • Plane • Sandpaper • Paintbrush

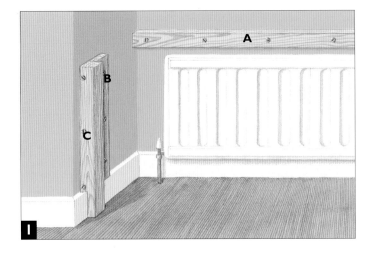

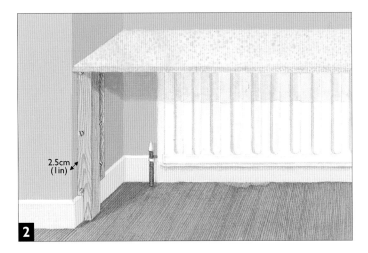

2 Measure the full height from the underside of the shelf to the floor. Cut two 5 x 5cm (2 x 2in) battens (C). These will fit to the front of B and need to be profiled to suit any skirting. Pre-drill and countersink holes close to the profiled end to attach C to B.

Measure the alcove for shelf size (no alcove is square, so check front, back and sides carefully). Measure the full depth of the alcove (the shelf will overhang the front upright posts (C) by 2.5cm [1in]). Cut a sheet of 2cm (¾in) MDF to this size. Pre-drill and countersink holes in the MDF, one above each C batten and the others spaced at 30cm (12in) intervals above batten A, then screw down.

1 Measure the width of the alcove and the height of the radiator plus 7.5cm (3in). This will be the height of the underside of the shelf. Cut one timber batten 7.5 x 2.5cm (3 x 1in) (A) to the width of the alcove. Pre-drill and countersink holes 4cm (1½in) in from each end, and 30cm (12in) apart. Using a spirit level, hold batten A against the wall, and when level, screw to the wall using wall plugs (mollies). Sitting the bottom of the front upright posts (5 x 2.5 cm [2 x 1in]) (B) on the skirting board and cutting them level with the height of A, screw in 7.5cm (3in) from the corner.

3 The height of the gates should be the distance from the floor to the underside of the shelf less 6mm (¼in) to allow for clearance top and bottom. The width of the gates is the distance

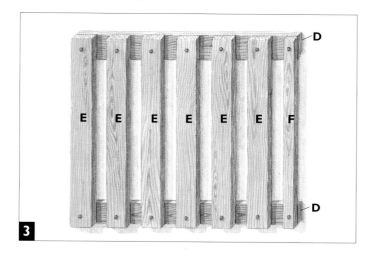

3

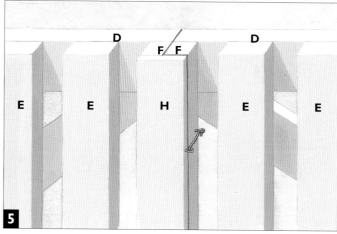

5

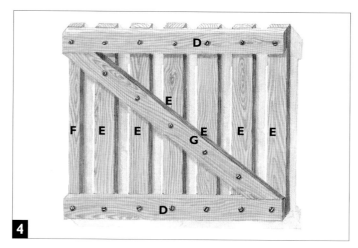

4

(1 x 1in) batten (F) for each gate. First lay two E battens on the horizontal D battens at the hinge side of each gate. Then lay the two F battens on the centre edges. Fix each strut top and bottom with glue and panel pins (nails). Fit the remaining E battens approx. 4cm (1½in) apart, and attach in the same way.

4 Turn the gates over and screw in at the back of each upright. Measure one length of 5 x 2.5cm (2 x 1in) batten (G) diagonally from the bottom hinge side to the top centre side. Cut at an angle to fit, then screw down.

5 With the front sides of the gates facing you, measure the central strut top to bottom and cut a length of 50 x 12mm (2 x ½in) batten (H). Glue and pin this to F as before on one gate only. This will mask both central struts. Hang both gates flush to struts (C) with brass butt hinges. Sand down any rough edges, and paint the gates with a coat of acrylic primer. Fill all screw and pin holes with wood filler, sand, then paint the gates and shelf with two coats of eggshell to suit the decoration of the room. Finally, fit a brass hook and eye, as shown.

between the upright posts (C) less an allowance of 6mm (¼in). Divide this measurement in half to get the width of each gate.

For each gate cut two lengths of 5 x 2.5cm (2 x 1in) batten (D) equal to the full width of the gate, and lay flat. Depending on the width of the gate, cut out the required amount of 5 x 2.5cm (2 x 1in) uprights (E) and a length of 2.5 x 2.5cm

CHAPTER TWO

DECORATING WITH FABRIC

AUTHENTIC FABRICS

Most people think of the fabric on chairs and upholstery in a Swedish interior as being checked or striped, with white muslin or cotton used as curtains. In some of the prettiest rooms, however, floral sprig-printed cottons are used in the French manner to delightful and dramatic effect. All the curtains and bed drapes are of the same fabric, including the upholstery. But it never looks overpowering because the overall look of the room is pared down, and the patterns on the fabrics are always delicate with sprigs of flowers sparingly scattered. Many of the fabrics are printed in one colour only: sepia brown printed on an off-white cotton or linen is hard to find but worth the search as it has a wonderfully restrained quality. Red, blue and green prints on off-white are more readily available and they too can look stunning.

When I first started to design using Swedish interiors as my inspiration there were hardly any checked fabrics on the market, so I had to use cotton gingham tablecloth material which I bought by the yard from a restaurant supplier. The only colours available at that stage were rather strong, but I used them in kitchens and bathrooms where they lent a rural feel to the overall look. The variety of checked fabric available today is enormous: you can even find soft, muted colours that are perfect for bedrooms, where I always use calm, receding tones, or a more formal interior, such as a sitting room or dining room.

Opposite above: The total composure of this bedroom in Skogaholm is the result of restraint in design: the placement of furniture is precise and symmetrical, and the same delicate sepia and off-white printed linen is used throughout. The sombre red-brown of the painted bed is lightened by the fabric of the half-tester which, although it almost touches the ceiling, still appears to be quite modest because the unlined hangings fall very simply. And the chairs are upholstered in the same fabric, further containing the unpretentious look.

Opposite below: Another bedroom in Skogaholm illustrates how a double-frilled dressing table cover and veiled mirror – an apparently excessive idea – can be made to look almost modest. The rest of the sparsely furnished room has quite a masculine feel, toning down the prettiness of the flounced fabrics. And a pair of formally placed candlesticks on the dressing table also stand firm against any feeling of sentimentality.

'Modest stripes and checks, clean white muslins and linens, and cottons with simple flower motifs – these are the basics.'

The Scandinavian obsession with letting in as much daylight as possible means that curtains should never be heavy and dark. Instead, white muslins should just fall delicately around the window, and cotton, linen or drawn-thread work curtains should be left unlined in order to allow light to filter through. All curtains should be easily washable and quick to rehang so that the room can stay as fresh and airily crisp as when it was first created.

Above: Despite the fact that it does not appear typically Swedish, the combination of the highly decorative chinoiserie walls and the large-scale green-and-white checked slip covers and curtains in the principal bedroom at Svindersvik was another source of inspiration for me.

Simple Curtain Solutions

I have fought for years against over-designed and elaborate curtains that overpower a room and are extravagantly expensive to make or have made; it seems to me far better, aesthetically speaking, and much cheaper too, to keep your curtains simple. In contrast, I have always liked the way the Swedish add a romantic touch to their typically scant curtains: the way they put a mere wisp of muslin or a simple cotton valance just to frame the window and let in as much daylight as possible.

Undoubtedly, the best way to recreate this look is to use antique linen. After year upon year of laundering, old linen falls beautifully, and the fine drawn-thread work and embroidery is generally of a very high quality. Dress up a window with a valance made of a table runner or the top of an antique sheet; either is perfect in its new role. Then use a roller blind behind the valance to control the light; it will be well hidden when not in use. Incidentally, off-white or cream blinds seem to look best.

Curtains that drop heavily to the floor have been fashionable for years, even on windows where shorter curtains would originally

I devised another way to use butter muslin to delightful effect when I was confronted by this small circular window in an attic bedroom. The fabric is simply folded over at the top to create its own valance and then sewn onto antiqued brass curtain rings and hung from a thin pole the size of a broomstick handle. Combined with a rose-red gingham roller blind behind, the finished effect is both charmingly romantic and freshly clean and uncluttered.

Left: Antique pillow shams, tablecloths or table runners, folded over and caught up with café clips, make simple but very effective no-sew curtains, with an integral valance at the top.

Right: These pretty red-and-white curtains lashed to a thin pole create a decorative frame for this window, hiding the unsightly mechanics at the top of the roller blind at the same time.

'Simple, unlined curtains let light in; elaborate curtains shut it out.'

have been hung. If your curtains fall to the ground, it is better not to make them too full; indeed, the less fabric the better. And although abundant flowery chintzes with top-heavy valances would undoubtedly look unsightly to the sill, when used in the right place, a lightweight, unlined cotton with a small gathered heading might look fresh and unassuming.

Many plain fabrics, including muslin and cotton, look best unlined, but you may have to help a patterned fabric by lining it, because when the light shines through it the design will be bleached out. I have often made checked curtains from tablecloth fabric; it is both cheerful and practical, washing well without shrinking, so that the curtains can be cleaned frequently to keep the atmosphere bright. But it is worth noting that Indian fabrics used for curtains must be pre-washed to avoid later shrinkage.

MUSLIN SWAG CURTAINS

There is nothing so romantic as white muslin curtains blowing in the breeze with the sun shining through them. Windows are for letting light in and, in the Swedish style, curtains are designed to control the light and not to block it out. Carl Larsson taught me to bring the outdoors indoors.

This project consists of one pair of slot-headed curtains on a pole with a piece of fabric draped over a larger pole to form a swag. The curtains under the muslin swag are drawn together at the top, but held back at window-sill height by decorative ombras (tiebacks). For screening of light and privacy, the ideal solution is to use a roller blind behind the curtains; the blind may be lined with blackout material for extra screening and insulation if you wish.

Muslin, lawn and fine cotton not only filter the light but will drape well over the pole; avoid fabrics that are too stiff. The muslin used in this project should first be washed to pre-shrink it and to remove the dressing. A white cotton bobble trim on the leading edge of the curtains softens the opening and makes the light dance through them even more.

It is important that the swag should look as though it has just been thrown over the pole, that the tails fall naturally and that the whole effect isn't too precise. In a Swedish-style room, curtains should not look over-designed and stand out in a self-conscious way; they should be a simple part of the whole design of the room.

Opposite: A red-and-white flower-sprigged cotton roller blind under curtains and swags of butter muslin serves to filter the daylight in the most romantic way.

Above: This small guest bedroom plays a double role; it is also used as a study. The red-brown painted desk in front of the window is a perfect place to work.

MUSLIN SWAG CURTAINS : PROJECT

YOU WILL NEED:
MATERIALS
2cm (¾ in) pole and brackets •
Larger pole and brackets •
Wood blocks • Screws • Muslin •
Thread • Bobble braid •
Two ombras (tiebacks)

TOOLS AND EQUIPMENT
Drill • Wall plugs (mollies) •
Tape measure • Dressmaking
scissors • Pins • Iron • Needles •
Sewing machine • Cord or
string • Pen • Paper

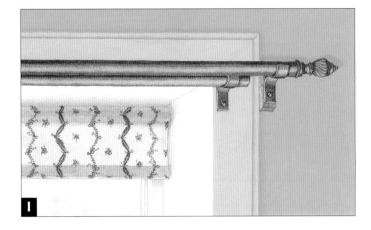

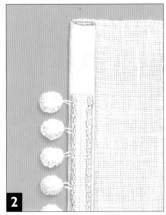

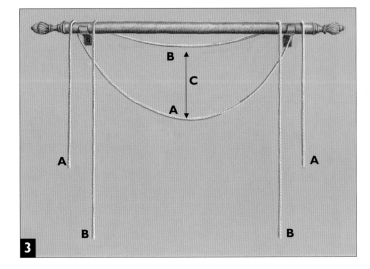

1 Decide on the best position for the roller blind, if you need one. The curtain should fall in front of the blind, with plenty of clearance. The pole for the swag needs to be in front of the curtains. Use wood blocks behind the brackets to achieve the clearance.

For the curtain drop, measure from the base of the smaller pole to the floor, adding 11cm (4½in) for the heading, 15cm (6in) for the hem and 12cm (4¾in) for the billowing effect when the curtains are draped back over the ombras (tiebacks). Use the full length of the pole to measure each curtain width, to give fullness.

2 Cut out the curtain material and cut off any selvage present. Fold, pin and press a double side hem of 1cm (⅜in) on the leading and outer edges of each curtain. Tack and machine stitch the outer edges. Pin and tack the bobble braid in the centre of the leading edge hems, leaving 11cm (4½in) at the top and 15cm (6in) at the bottom clear of braid. Machine stitch in place. Turn up a double hem of 7.5cm (3in) on each cur-

tain and then press, tack and machine stitch.

For the slot headings, turn down 1cm (⅜in) and press, then turn down a further 5cm (2in) and press. Stitch 1cm (⅜in) from the top fold,

then stitch very close to the bottom edge (see page 61). Insert the 2cm (⅜in) pole through the curtains and hang them, catching them open on two ombras (tiebacks) placed at suitable

3 Place the larger pole on its brackets. Cut two very long lengths of cord or string. Drape both over the pole, one to represent the outside edge of the swag (A) and one to represent the inner edge (B). Alter the length and depth of the swag until the proportions look right. Mark the pole and the cords in the four spots where they touch and cut the cords where you want the swag tails to end. Measure and note down the swag depth (C).

4 On some large sheets of paper, draw a straight line the length of B, multiply measurement C by 2.5 and draw it in at right angles centred on B; then draw in a straight line the length of A, centred on and at right angles to C. Join up A and B. Transfer the pen marks on the cords and draw lines between them to show where the swag will be gathered.

Using this pattern, cut the swag on the grain (so that C runs across the width of the

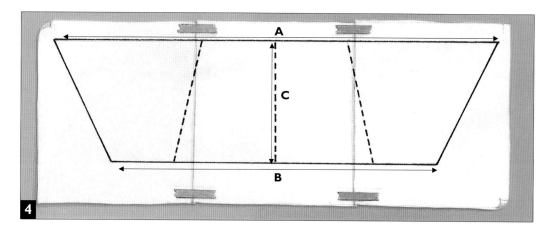

fabric). If C is almost the same width as the fabric, use the whole width, and benefit from not having to hem the selvaged edges. Otherwise, pin, tack and hand stitch in a double hem of 1cm (⅜in) at top and bottom. Leave the tail ends unhemmed. Tack along the gathering lines using a matching thread, then pull the threads to gather the swag loosely.

5 Make a base to stitch the swag to by 'lagging' the pole with slip-stitched bands of muslin in the two places between the pen marks. Position the gathers of the swag over these lagged areas.

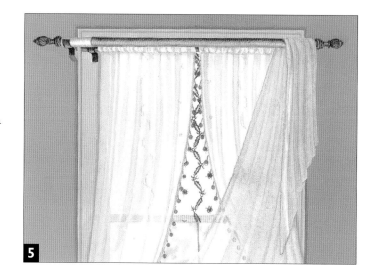

Pull the top edge of the swag (the B edge) to meet the underside of the pole. Tuck any excess material into the back of the gathers and stitch into place. Use your fingers to stroke the folds into a natural arrangement, then loosely hand stitch the swag on to the muslin bands. Leave the swag ends raw, cutting them very cleanly on the cross to make a pleasing final shape.

SLOT-HEADED CURTAINS

I achieved the calm and tranquil quality of this pretty bedroom by using the same checked fabric on the walls and for the curtains. This potentially busy look is lightened by the pale, painted panelling and the antique cream embroidered bedspread. With so much going on in the room, it was necessary to use an extremely simple curtain treatment and this slot heading and valance is quick and easy to achieve. Wide antique lace at the edge of standard roller blinds softens the look and filters the light beautifully.

These unlined slot-headed curtains and valance are an example of a very typical Swedish device. They are so easy to make because just two rows of stitching create the slot heading that allows the curtains and valance to be slipped on to the one pole.

This style of curtain is usually made up in white muslin, cotton or linen and is particularly well suited to simple patterned fabrics, such as this checked linen. Creamy antique French linen sheets also work well as they tend to fall beautifully and, with the light behind them, have a wonderful golden glow. A linen, such as the one used here, works best for long curtains; it needs the weight of a full-length curtain to fall properly, and would 'bounce' if shorter. Muslin, however, can equally well be used for floor-length curtains.

It is important to establish from the outset how the width of the window is to be divided into curtain and valance areas. For this project the curtains hang over the outer two-thirds of the width, and the valance over the central third. You should, however, make your own judgement about this proportion, bearing in mind the shape of the window and the angle of the drape effect you require when the curtains are tied back.

As these curtains do not close fully, a roller blind beneath the valance is necessary to control the light and to provide privacy. The curtains and valance need to stand away from the roller blind so that it can be used without danger of getting caught in the valance.

SLOT-HEADED CURTAINS : PROJECT

YOU WILL NEED:

MATERIALS

2cm (¾in) curtain pole and brackets • Wood blocks • Curtain fabric • Thread • Tie-back holders • Screws • Ribbon tie-backs

TOOLS AND EQUIPMENT

Drill • Wall plugs (mollies) • Tape measure • Scissors • Iron • Pins • Needles • Sewing machine • Screwdriver

I Fix up the brackets and pole directly above the architrave of the window (if there is one), on wood blocks if the pole needs to be away from a roller blind. Calculate the drop of the curtain material by measuring from the base of the pole to the floor, adding 20cm (8in) for the hem and 13cm (5⅛in) for the heading. Calculate the width of each curtain by measuring the pole, doubling it for fullness, and dividing this measurement by three (one per curtain and one for the valance). Cut out the two curtains, checking that their patterns match.

Now calculate the drop of the valance material – 15 per cent of the length of the curtains is usually about right – adding 4cm (1⅛in) for the hem and 13cm (5⅛in) for the heading. Make sure the valance pattern-repeat matches that of the curtains.

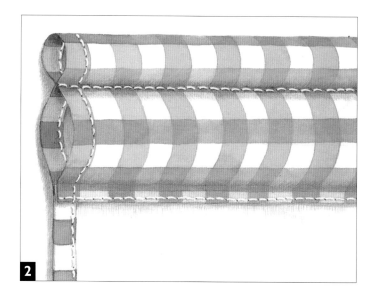

2

3

2 Lay both pieces of curtain fabric face down and pin double side hems of 2cm (¾in), ensuring that whole checks or stripes are visible at the edges. Press these turnings, tack and machine stitch them close to the inner edges. Turn up a double hem of 10cm (4in) at the bases of the fabric lengths, checking that the folds are at right angles to the side turnings and so don't protrude at the sides.

For the headings, turn over the top 6mm (¼in) and press. Turn down a further 6.5cm (2½in) and press again. Then stitch along 2cm (¾in) down from the top folds, to form a shallow frill above the pole, and a further 4cm (1½in) down to create the slotted headings.

Now turn in the sides of the valance material by 6mm (¼in) and press them, then turn them in by a further 2.5cm (1in), press again, tack and machine stitch. Turn up a double hem of 2.5cm (1in) and machine stitch. Make up the top heading of the valance in exactly the same way as for the curtains.

3 Using scissors, cut one slot on the back of each curtain heading, approximately 7.5cm (3in) in from the outer edge, aligning them with the brackets. Slide the valance onto the pole, and then a curtain at each side. The cut slots of the curtains sit in front of the brackets, allowing the remaining end of each curtain to be slipped over the end of the pole. If your pole has finials, screw them in place now.

Screw two small tie-back holders to the wall at dado height, sill height, or a height that seems particularly suitable to the proportions of the room, and tie back the curtains. (Experiment first by holding the curtains back at various heights before deciding on the position of the tie-back holders.) In this example Petersham ribbon was used for the tie-backs.

ROLLER BLIND WITH LACE TRIM

Roller blinds are particularly useful in combination with curtains that don't close. You can either buy perfectly serviceable ready-made plain Holland blinds or else buy a kit and use the fabric of your choice – checked and sprigged cottons can be very successful.

I frequently add a wide trimming of lace to the bottom edge of my blinds; this 'ages' them and creates a beautiful play of light. Antique lace can be expensive when bought by the yard, so I recommend buying old household linen and removing the lace. If you can only find new lace, dye it to a pale cream colour in a weak tea solution.

Divide up very wide windows with a number of long, narrow blinds; this improves the window's proportions, avoids a wide blind going up awkwardly and gives greater control of the light.

YOU WILL NEED:
MATERIALS
Ready-made roller blind (or kit with your own choice of fabric) • Fabric stiffener (taking particular note of ventilation instructions) • Lace (at least 7.5cm [3in] wide) • Fabric adhesive or double-sided tape

TOOLS AND EQUIPMENT
Tape measure • Scissors

I Measure the width of the blind. Remove the wooden batten and any pull fixings from the bottom edge.

2 Cut the lace to the same width (any pattern symmetrically placed). Lay it along the back of the blind, its top edge covering the line of machine stitching which forms the hem.

3 Stick the lace down with good fabric adhesive that dries transparent or with double-sided tape (which lasts about a year). Spray with fabric stiffener. Replace the wooden batten and any pull fixings. Hang your blind in position.

The hard-edged effect of an off-the-peg roller blind can be completely transformed simply by edging it with lace. Saved from a worn-out tablecloth, perhaps, or a pillow sham, the wide strip of lace creates a beautiful play of light.

I have always been fascinated by Swedish rustic boxed-in beds, which are often built into the corner of the room and enclosed on all sides but one. On the open side there is a decorative cut-out in the wooden panel, presumably to prevent draughts, and a simple curtain is then drawn across the opening at night, which almost turns the bed into a room of its own. This is a wonderful traditional idea for a child's room today, or for a room that has two uses. And if I were to recreate this private yet cosy look in a bedroom, I would use a white damask or homespun cotton bedspread, with pillows in a mixture of checked cotton and antique white pillowcases, and a simple gingham curtain.

In a more formal bedroom I would use a half-tester, but with a very simple, unlined flower-sprigged cotton for the hangings and valance, which would match the window curtains. Using the same fabric throughout a room never looks overpowering if a one-colour print on an off-white cotton is used (see pages·50-1). For a harder-edged look, I might dress the bed with a painted headboard with lots of pillows: continental square pillows in a

'In the right proportions and fabrics, Swedish-style bed drapes look pretty but not sentimental.'

Opposite above: One of the bedrooms at the Drottningholm Court Theatre. Half the charm of this very elegant tall room is the green-and-white checked bed linen with very simple drapes. Checks abound in Sweden and are used for everything; they will give any scheme a simple look.

Opposite below: This high cut-out bed is a very typical Swedish shape. Hunt out antique embroidered bed linen like the pretty, cross-stitched valance here to create your own rustic look.

Right: This simple canopied bed with unlined blue-and-white linen curtains and white embroidered bedspread is charmingly naïve.

simple check at the back, with smaller pillows in antique white pillowslips (or modern copies) in front of them, and finally a couple of little embroidered cushions. Remember to keep paring it down to avoid overdressing the bed.

If you have a single bed, place it sideways against a wall and it will offer you the chance to hang drapes above it, which can look wonderful. And if it is not in the corner of the room, the bed will need a headboard or it will be uncomfortable (see page 38).

Traditionally, the draped canopy needed a timber frame to support the fabric, but I have developed a more simplified version. I use long lengths of white muslin, checked gingham or striped cotton draped over a central ombra (tieback), with two more ombras (tiebacks), one at each end of the bed, to hold the fabric back in swags. Not only is this an elegant visual solution – and wonderfully authentic too – it is also easy and inexpensive to construct oneself. With bolsters at each end, a bed has found a new role as a day bed.

HALF-TESTER WITH HANGINGS

The Scandinavians simplified every aspect of formal European interior design; instead of making a tester of gilded wood and silk hangings, for instance, they preferred the more restrained effect of painted wood and printed cotton. The drama of the tester in this project comes not from the sumptuousness of its materials, but from its carefully judged proportions. It is only 20cm (8in) deep, so would not be out of place in a normal-sized bedroom, but is nevertheless very high, nearly touching the ceiling. The height of a tester should be determined by the proportions of the room. Before starting to make one, stand back and consider whether it should be higher or lower than the tops of the windows, and, if there is a picture rail, whether it should align with this. A rough scale drawing can be very useful in helping you determine the best height; often the decision will be made for you once the dimensions are down on paper. The half-tester shown here is 2.6m (8ft 6in) long, and the valance drop is 30cm (12in) long. You will need to judge these proportions by eye if your tester is at a different height.

The tester consists of a simple cornice shape: a flat piece of chipboard, skirted on three sides by decorative moulding, and treated with antiquing wax. The hangings consist of four lengths of material: a gathered back panel, a valance and two side curtains, all of which are unlined for a light, unfussy look.

Opposite: The half-tester is very dramatic because it nearly touches the ceiling. By using a simple, one-colour printed cotton, the look is kept very spare. And painting the cornice of the pelmet the same colour as the painted, panelled wall, keeps the total look modest and restrained.

Above: I wanted this bedroom to have an ethereal quality. The painted, panelled walls are the palest of greys with pink motifs painted so lightly that they are hardly there. The furniture I designed is all very delicate, and again is painted in the palest grey. The blue of the half-tester fabric tones with the grey so that the room is almost monochrome except for the pink in the fabric of the stool at the end of the bed.

HALF-TESTER WITH HANGINGS : PROJECT

YOU WILL NEED:

MATERIALS

Sheet of 12mm (½in) chipboard, measuring the width of your bed x 20cm (8in) • 7.5 x 2.5cm (3 x 1in) batten • 7-7.5cm (2¾-3in) wooden moulding • Wood glue • Panel pins (nails) • Acrylic primer • Wood filler • Matt vinyl paint • Antiquing wax • Screws • Wall plugs (mollies) • Fabric for back panel, curtains and valance • Thread • Narrow heading tape

TOOLS AND EQUIPMENT

Tape measure • Straight edge • Panel saw • Drill • Drill bits to suit gauge of screws and countersink bit • Mitre block • Hammer • Nail punch • Sandpaper • 4cm (1½in) decorating brush • Lint-free rags • Spirit level • Bradawl • Screwdriver • Dressmaking scissors • Iron • Pins • Needle • Sewing machine • Staple gun and upholstery tacks

Drill and countersink screw holes 12mm (½in) in from the back edge of the 12mm (½in) sheet of chipboard at approx. 25cm (10in) intervals, centred on the width, finishing 6cm (2¼in) in from the sides. This will form the tester top.

For the back support strut cut a length of batten to the same length as the top, less 4cm (1½in). Drill and countersink holes approx. every 25cm (10in) along the batten, ensuring that they are offset with the holes drilled on the tester top.

Measure and cut sufficient moulding to skirt the three projecting sides of the top, allowing for mitring of the front corners, then mitre the corners in a mitre block (see page 37). Fix the moulding in place with glue and panel pins (nails), driving the pins below the surface of the moulding with a nail punch.

Sand off any rough edges then paint the entire tester with acrylic primer. Fill any holes (except pre-drilled

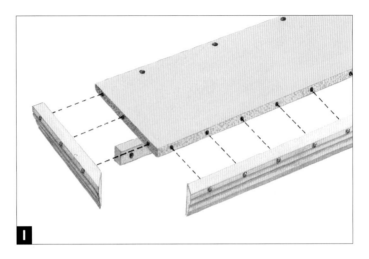

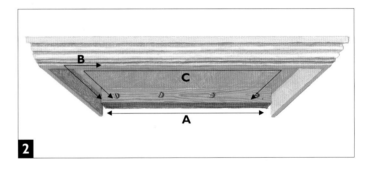

screw holes), sand down and paint with two coats of matt vinyl. Treat with antiquing wax (see page 93). Paint the support batten the same colour as the walls, and, using a spirit level – and the calculated length of the curtains (see step 2) – place it in position on the wall. Using a bradawl and ham-

mer, mark the position of the holes on the wall by tapping through each hole in turn. Put the batten to one side and drill the holes in the wall, insert wall plugs (mollies), then screw the batten into position. Centre the tester on this batten and screw down.

2 To cut the hangings, start with the back panel. Establish its width by doubling the inside width of the pelmet (A) for fullness. Its drop is the length from the underside of the pelmet top to the floor plus 2.5cm (1in) for the heading and 20cm (8in) for the hem. Cut out this back panel, joining two widths if necessary.

For each curtain width, measure the inside depth of the pelmet, adding 23cm (9in) for the front return (B) and double this measurement for fullness. The drop and heading and hem allowances will be the same as for the back panel. Cut out the two curtains.

For the valance, measure the inside width and depths of the three projecting sides of the tester (C) and double this measurement for fullness. The drop in this project will be 30cm (12in) plus a 2.5cm (1in) heading allowance and 10cm (4in) for the hem. Cut out the fabric for the valance.

3 To make the hangings, turn and pin double side hems of 2cm (¾in) and a double bottom hem of 10cm (4in) on the back panel, pressing, tacking and stitching close to the inner edge. Repeat this process for the two curtains and valance, except turning a double 5cm (2in) bottom hem on the latter.

Turn down the top 2.5cm (1in) of the back panel on the wrong side and press, then place heading tape 6mm (¼in) in from the top fold, turn under the ends, and tack and stitch the tape along its top and bottom edges. For the curtains and valance turn down a 2.5cm (1in) fold on the right side of the fabric and stitch on the heading tape as before.

4 Gather the valance to fit C. First, fix it to the inside of the two front corners using a staple gun, then tuck the back corners between the support batten and the moulding and finally

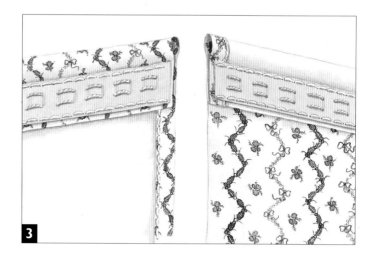

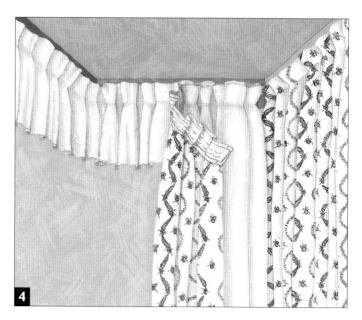

staple up along its entire width. Now gather the back panel and staple along the length of A, tucking in the ends as for the valance. Gather each side curtain to measurement B and staple up as before.

CHAIR CUSHION

This is a modern version of original Swedish slip covers, as found in Carl Larsson's paintings, which consisted simply of a piece of material cut to shape and tied as protection over expensive upholstery. Today, as tied-on chair seat cushions, they can dress up an ordinary country chair, introduce a dash of colour, or else, if made in fabrics that match the rest of the soft furnishings, pull together the look of a room. These cushions are so adaptable and easily changed that you could consider having a summer set and a winter set for seasonal variety.

It is important that loose covers of any sort should be easy to clean, so I am inclined to use linens and cottons and other machine-washable fabrics. It is always wise to give the fabric a wash first in order to avoid any later shrinkage; equally, the piping should be pre-shrunk by being placed in a pillow case and machine-washed at a high temperature.

Most loose covers are made up with the pattern or stripe of the fabric running from the back to the front and the design on the front frill running in the same direction. The tie-ends can have the stripes running either lengthwise or across the width of the fabric. I tend to make these ends very long because then they can be wound around the chair leg and tied at the bottom, which both looks very pretty and secures them well. They are reminiscent of those in Carl Larsson's own home

Opposite: Slip covers – cut to shape, laid over the chair and tied at the legs to stop them slipping – would originally have been used to protect a more expensive fabric.

Above: One of Carl Larsson's illustrations was the inspiration for this chair. The blue-and-white fabric looks especially fresh against the off-white and yellow ochre.

CHAIR CUSHION : PROJECT

YOU WILL NEED:

MATERIALS

Dining chair • Washed and
ironed cushion fabric • Sewing
thread • Pre-shrunk piping –
5mm (³⁄₁₆in) diameter • Ready-
made feather cushion

TOOLS AND EQUIPMENT

Large sheet of tracing paper •
Pencil • Scissors • Pins • Tape
measure • Tailor's chalk •
Needle • Iron • Sewing
machine

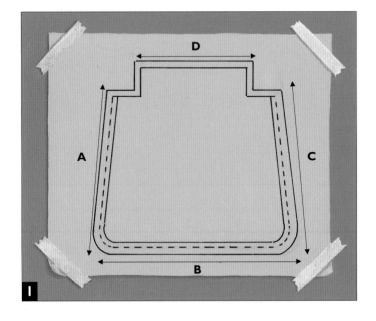

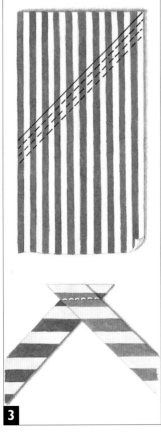

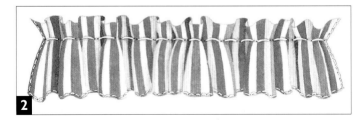

1 Make a tracing of the chair seat (including the chair struts). Add 12mm (½in) to the width and the length for fullness. Round off the front corners on the tracing then add a 1.5cm (⅝in) seam allowance all round. Cut out the pattern and pin it to the cushion fabric. Cut out two identical pieces.

2 Two strips of fabric are required for the frill. To make the pattern, decide on the depth you want then add to this 1.5cm (⅝in) for the seam allowance and 4cm (1½in) for the hem. The amount of fabric needed for the first strip is the total measurement of A, B and C multiplied by 1.5 for fullness, plus 6cm (2¼in) for side turnings (this may need to have a seam). For the second strip (the back frill length) multiply measurement D by 1.5, plus 6cm (2¼in).

Cut out the two strips, turn up a double hem of 2cm (¾in) along their lengths and a double hem of 1.5cm (⅝in) at each side, and press, tack and machine stitch them. Mark the longer piece of fabric into three sections with tailor's chalk and gather the sections evenly with a loose machine stitch or by hand along the seam line, 1.5cm (⅝in) from the top, until they reach the required lengths (A, B and C). Gather the shorter piece to its required length (D) and set both pieces aside.

3 To establish the length of piping required, measure around A, B, C and D (including the chair strut holes) on the paper pattern and add about 7cm (2¾in). To make the piping cover, fold the fabric on the diagonal (the bias), press a crease into it, then cut as many 5cm (2in) wide strips as you require parallel to this crease. These strips may be joined by being placed at 90 degrees, right sides together, stitched at 45 degrees corner to corner and trimmed. Wrap the fabric around the cord and pin and tack very close to it, trying to keep a 1.5cm (⅝in) seam allowance

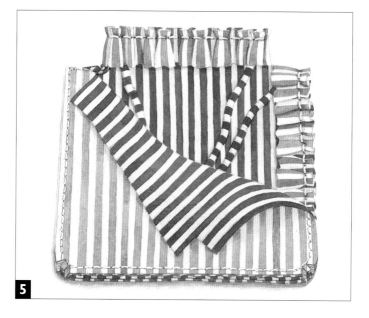

4 For the tie-ends cut out four strips of fabric 3cm (1³⁄₁₆in) wide and 90cm (3ft) long. Turn in both ends of each strip and machine stitch small hems. Fold in the raw edges, fold the strips in half and then machine stitch lengthwise.

5 To sew the cushion together, start by pinning the piping all the way round the right side of one of the cover pieces, starting at the centre of the back, with the raw edges of the piping fabric aligning with the raw edge of the cushion fabric. (You will need to clip the seam allowance on the piping when you go round corners, particularly the angular ones of the struts, to ensure a good fit.) Where the piping joins at the back, trim the cord and cover to overlap slightly, then stitch the cord ends then the cover together. Tack then machine stitch as close to the piping as you can, using a piping foot. Now tack the ties over the piping at either side of the chair struts, their long ends towards the centre.

Lay the two strips of frill, right sides down, on top of the piping, matching the seam allowances. The frill hem will be towards the centre of the cushion. (Again, you will need to clip the corners.) Pin and tack along the seam line, 1.5cm (⅝in) in from the raw edges. Now lie the bottom cover over the top with right sides together. Pin and tack 1.5cm (⅝in) in from the raw edge, aligning the seam allowances all round the cushion. Now turn the cover over and machine stitch the line of the piping (still using the piping foot), going over the ties twice but leaving a slot 2.5cm (1in) in from either end of D.

Turn the cushion cover right side out, then insert the cushion. Finally, slip stitch the opening to seal it.

CHAPTER THREE

COLOUR AND PAINT

COLOUR IN INTERIORS

The Swedish palette is fundamentally dependent on that famous clear, northern light that features so strongly in all Scandinavian design, and it would be impossible to reproduce it exactly in another environment. Remember that no matter how good your choice of colours in one location, the same might not work at all in another setting: a south-facing room, for instance, will light up colours in quite a different way from a north-facing one. So it is vital to try out quite large colour samples *in situ*, and to experiment on at least two walls, as each will reflect the light differently. The best way to understand colour is to use it.

The colours that comprise the Swedish palette are generally pale, though sometimes punctuated by stronger, muted greens, blues and reds. Authentic colours are often still made up from traditional recipes and natural pigments, and this gives them a wonderful, distinctive quality. But they do take a lot of time to mix and, in the past, they often contained lead, which would nowadays make them too dangerous to use. It is much safer and easier to buy off-the-shelf paints; the range is now so enormous that I always find what I want. The key is to buy a large selection of sample tins and to test out the colours first. Greens are possibly the easiest colours because you can often find exactly the right shade ready-mixed. Blues look more subtle with a touch of raw umber added to them. I always avoid whites and beiges 'with a hint of pink', preferring a

'Fancy paint finishes are not necessary – all you need is to find the right colour and to use a matt finish.'

cooler, greenish hue; but warm greys are usually better than those with a blue tinge, which can look very cold.

The patina of the most attractive painted surfaces is never shiny but rather has a soft, natural sheen from years of wear. As a general rule, then, keep the paint as matt as possible. But to recreate this look I often put on two coats of eggshell, making the final coat one of flat oil. The eggshell underneath has the added advantage of keeping the surface reasonably hard-wearing; flat matt paint is not so tough. I am myself still playing with colour; I am constantly amazed by its infinite ability to surprise.

Opposite: My design for this little girl's bedroom had its roots in Swedish boxed-in beds. As always, I used a raw umber wash to tone down strong blues and age whites.

Above: In contrast to the matt walls, the soft sheen of the planked floors gently reflects the light, and draws the eye right back to the chalky-coloured room beyond.

Above: The delicate, muted blue of these wooden stairs leading to an attic bedroom was created simply by adding raw umber to a ready-mixed colour. A plastered wall has

been chiselled to look like tongue-and-groove cladding, and painted a soft green, so that it is hard to tell that it is not the real thing.

MIXING COLOURS AND PIGMENTS

The pale receding colours of Scandinavia lend any interior a sense of calm: there are off-whites, pale greys, soft, muted greens, pale yellow ochres, blues with a greenish hue, pure pale blues and a wonderful rusty red – though this is generally used for exteriors.

It is no longer difficult to find the right colours to achieve the Swedish look because there are so many standard paint colours now available. If you are determined, you can usually find the one you want. Beware of deceptive shade cards, however: the patches of colour are so small that it is impossible to visualize the large effect. Instead, to get a more accurate impression, it is better to 'invest', buying a wide variety of little test pots and painting larger pieces of paper or scraps of wood.

If you cannot find the exact match for the muted colour you want, choose a colour that is stronger and brighter than you need and then make it paler by knocking down the colour with a touch of raw umber. This is what I call my magic potion. Raw umber is a brown pigment with a greenish tinge that never fails to knock back a colour to achieve the more characteristic muted tones of Swedish interior design: blues will become greener; greens will look softer and more aged; whites will look older, touched by a soft greeny-grey; yellow ochres will mellow; and reds will lose their brashness.

If you buy raw umber as a powder pigment – and do not confuse it with burnt umber, which is a reddish brown – it will need

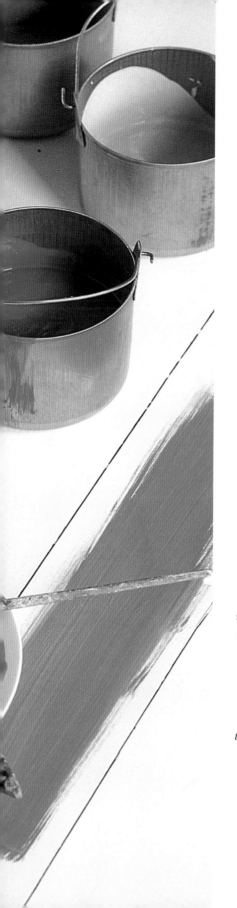

Above: Raw umber is the magic potion; added to any colour it will add a soft, muted quality – essential for achieving an authentic Swedish interior. In its original state it is a natural powder pigment, like ochre but darker and browner, with a greenish hue. It should not be confused with burnt umber, which is redder.

Left: This is a typically Swedish palette, different shades of off-white combined with intense yet muted colours. If you cannot find the exact shade you are searching for, choose a brighter, stronger colour, and add white and a touch of raw umber to tone it down. Shown here is a mid-blue that has been 'doctored' using this method. Always ensure that the paints are thoroughly mixed to avoid unsightly streaks.

'Add raw umber to your paints to achieve the muted, Swedish-style palette.'

to be very well mixed with a drop of the appropriate wetting agent before being added to the paint, or you will be left with tiny beads of undissolved pigment which will cause streaks. It is far easier to buy the pigment ready dissolved, although even then, you should ensure that the raw umber is thoroughly mixed into the paint before use. You can buy it either in the form of a universal stainer, which will mix with either oil- or water-based paints and which is available from specialist decorating shops, or else as an artist's acrylic paint. This latter, though, is only suitable for use with water-based paints.

In order to judge how much raw umber to add, experiment by mixing small quantities of the pigment to the base colour on a plate and then in a jam jar; this should give you an idea of the proportions required. Then paint a corner of the room and watch carefully how the changing light through the day affects the colour. When you have finalized the colour you want, and need to mix the larger batch of paint, make sure you mix enough – not just for the job itself, but with some left over for later touch-ups – and add the pigment gradually in very small amounts until you reach the required hue. Remember: it is always possible to add a little more pigment, but if you add too much too fast, you will have wasted both paint and pigment, not to mention your time.

FLOORS

Floors play a major role in Swedish interiors, the most typical being wide floorboards, usually of pine. Scandinavians are very sensible about conserving heat and tend to use underfloor insulation so that the boards can be left bare without being cold and in order to prevent nasty draughts from coming up through them. Typically, floorboards are aged to a silvery blond through years of scrubbing and waxing. To reproduce this effect more quickly: wash the floor with a watered-down paint of off-white vinyl matt, then wipe it with a cotton rag to remove some of the colour (to stop it from looking too white), then varnish and finally wax it. Alternatively, apply a ready-mixed lime wax to the floor (as if you were polishing it), but this must be rubbed down very thoroughly or the white will come off on your shoes. Use wax sparingly and this will be less of a problem, and the floor will not look 'limed', just pale.

Another delightful Scandinavian device, reminiscent of seventeenth-century Dutch painting, is what I call modest marble tiling: pale diamond or square patterns painted directly onto the floorboards. In a formal room I would tend to use a diamond pattern in an off-white and pale khaki, but in a kitchen or bathroom I would be more inclined to paint squares of strong but muted blues and off-whites (see page 83).

You can paint the floor completely, of course, either off-white or else in a receding colour, such as a greeny-grey or a greeny-

beige. And painted floorboards can look particularly good with cotton or rag runners – long, narrow rugs with striped, checked or multicoloured but modest designs. As usual, check that the colours and design work with your overall scheme before you invest.

If, however, you prefer to have a carpet, choose a flat weave rather than a pile. Natural floor coverings such as seagrass, coir or jute are best because of their neutral colours and flat appearance. Always collect as many swatches as you can – and suppliers abound today – and try them out with the other colours you are using.

The sense of space that exudes from Swedish interiors is accentuated by the expanse of floor visible through the delicate legs of the furniture, and so skirted sofas and armchairs should be kept to a minimum. And the light and airy atmosphere is enhanced by the hard-edged quality of timber floors.

'The large expanse of floor visible in Swedish interiors creates light and space.'

Opposite left: 'Modest marble tiling', as I call it, is reminiscent of the black-and-white floors in seventeenth-century Dutch paintings. I find pale khaki-and-white diamond patterns work very well in halls and formal areas.

Opposite right: Long, thin rag rugs running around a room and flipped over at the corners are a typically Swedish touch. Not only do they protect the painted floorboards, but they soften the hard-edged look of the room too.

Right: Simple pine floorboards have been polished here with a ready-mixed lime wax to create a pale floor — so well loved and so widely used by the Swedish. The light in this sunny workplace is reflected beautifully by the floor. The geraniums on the window sill, red gingham curtains and a red, country-style chair are all typical ingredients of a Carl Larsson illustration.

CHEQUERED FLOOR

A painted floor should always be designed and planned in conjunction with the other features of a room since what might initially appear to be a simple painting job actually involves several practical and aesthetic decisions. Consider how the room is to be used, its size, and where the furniture will be placed, the colours of the walls and of the types of fabrics used, and, of course, the nature of the floor itself, including the condition and width of the floorboards. Once you have done this you should be in a position to decide whether a painted treatment is appropriate, and which colours you wish to use.

It is important that the scale of the chequerboard design be sympathetic to the proportions of the room. As a guide, a smallish room of approximately 3.35 x 3.35m (11 x 11ft) can take 15-20cm (6-8in) squares, and a larger room 20-30cm (8-12in) squares. It is very important that the painted squares never fall at the gap lines of the floorboards as there is nothing worse than beautiful sharp squares falling on fuzzy edges; it is essential, however, that the squares run parallel to the floorboards. Careful planning will ensure that your chequerboard squares span the floorboard gaps: you may need to adjust the size of the squares to achieve this. Once the painting is finished, a finish of polyurethane is ideal to seal the floor: hard-wearing semi-gloss coats may be used beneath a final, attractive (but less durable) matt coat.

If you have neither the time nor the inclination to mix your own paint, you should be able to find a pre-mixed paint the colour you want. Buy test pots first, however.

Emulsion (latex) is good for testing; it is cheaper and dries faster. Bear in mind that the protective polyurethane of varnish will yellow any colour slightly.

CHEQUERED FLOOR : PROJECT

PREPARATION

- Check for loose floorboards and any nails or screws sticking out. Hammer or screw them down.

- Vacuum and wash the floor to remove all dirt and grease.

- Use paint stripper to remove any old paint or varnish.

- If the floorboards are bare apply one coat of primer and then sand down.

YOU WILL NEED:
MATERIALS
Test pots of emulsion (latex) •
Acrylic primer undercoat •
White topcoat • Blue topcoat
(or colour of your choice) •
Semi-gloss polyurethane varnish
• Matt polyurethane varnish

TOOLS AND EQUIPMENT
Tape measure • Graph paper •
Pencil • Ruler • Large sheets
of paper • Two 5cm (2in)
paintbrushes • Sandpaper •
Vacuum cleaner • Floor cloths •
Turps or white spirit • Steel rule
• Coloured chalk • Set square
(triangle) • Masking tape •
2.5cm (1in) paintbrush •
Two artist's oil brushes

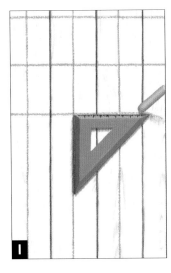

1

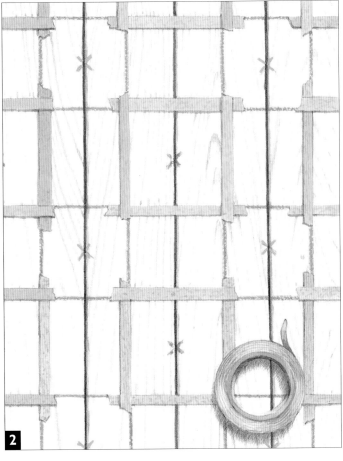

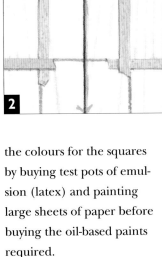

2

1 Measure your room and draw it to scale on graph paper. If you cannot fit an entire sequence of squares because the room is not square, decide which is the most important floor edge visually and establish a full row of squares here. Try out the colours for the squares by buying test pots of emulsion (latex) and painting large sheets of paper before buying the oil-based paints required.

Now apply a first layer of undercoat paint to the floor with the 5cm (2in) paint- brush, and leave it to dry overnight. (By painting in either the afternoon or evening, and leaving the paint to dry overnight, it is possible to retain daytime access to the room.) Lightly sand the floor down, vacuum up any dust and apply a second coat of undercoat, repeating the same process. Wipe the floor with a damp cloth. Clean the large brush in turps or white spirit and use it to paint the floor with two coats of the white top-coat, leaving each to dry overnight.

Next, using a steel rule and pale coloured chalk, mark out the lines parallel to the floorboards, then draw up the right-angled lines using a set square (triangle) to make the squares. Mark the squares that will be blue with a cross to avoid painting two next to each other.

2 Stick masking tape around the outer edge of alternate rows of blue squares (you can't paint all the blue squares at once because the masking tape will overlap the intervening squares that will be blue), also mask the skirting board and wall edge. This system also has the advantage of separating wet squares, thus preventing them from bleeding.

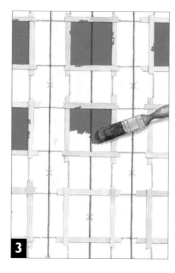

3 Use the smaller paint-brush to apply the blue paint within the masked areas. Make sure that the paint doesn't get too thick at the edges, otherwise it might bleed under the tape. Leave overnight to dry, then care-fully remove the tape. If any paint at the edges of the squares has bled, don't worry because the edges can easily be touched up later when the design is complete. Remember to keep a small amount of both your paints to one side for this purpose, (particularly if you have mixed a colour specially).

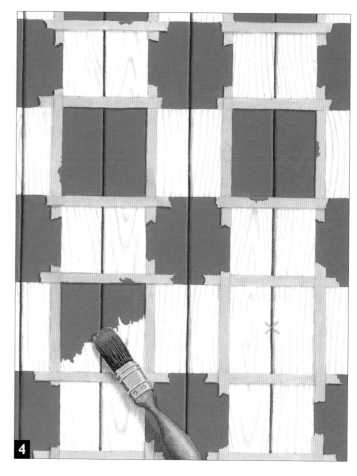

4 Now mask and paint the remaining blue squares in the same way and, once they are dry, remove the tape. Use the artist's brushes (one for the white, one for the blue) to touch up any areas that have bled under the tape.

Use the other 5cm (2in) paintbrush to paint the floor with three coats of semi-gloss polyurethane varnish and one coat of matt, which will yellow the white squares to a warmer antique-like hue. Leave 24 hours' drying time between each of the coats.

PAINTED WALL DECORATION

Inspired by the walls of Ekensberg Manor, Lake Mälaren, this painted wall decoration resonates with French influence – pared down in true Swedish style. Blues can be combined just as well in the bedroom as in displays of china; the lamp and bed are two different blues and the gingham bed linen introduces a third.

The Swedes looked upon painted wall decoration as an inexpensive and successful way of recreating something of the decorative richness of French interiors, and produced their own quintessentially Swedish adaptations of the rococo style. Their designs were more spare – a rococo festoon might be simplified to a few flowers gathered by a naïvely painted bow – and the colour palette notably more restrained. The wall paintings were rarely overpowering and have a wonderfully confident, fluid quality.

Most Swedish painted wall decoration was executed on linen stretched over wooden frames or tacked straight to the wall. The painted decoration in this project is executed straight on to the wall for the sake of practicality, but its principles remain the same: a restrained palette of receding colours; a simple design; the images painted with a very light touch; and the panels elongated by a low dado rail – only 40cm (approximately 16in) high.

This project's design was derived from the decorations on the walls of Ekensberg Manor near Lake Mälaren. I haven't aimed to reproduce how they might have looked in their original state, but rather to capture something of their current mellow, aged quality.

If the painted image is too strong you may find that the whole room has to be designed around it, but if the motifs are painted as slight impressions you will have far more scope for the fabrics and patterns of the furnishings.

PAINTED WALL DECORATION : PROJECT

PREPARATION

- Fix to the wall a moulding of about 4cm (1½in) to form a narrow dado rail roughly 40cm (16in) from the floor.
- Ensure that the walls are smooth: fill and sand down any uneven areas.

YOU WILL NEED:
MATERIALS
White matt vinyl emulsion (latex) • Artist's acrylic paint: raw umber, Prussian blue, black, burnt sienna, white • Four shades of grey matt vinyl emulsion (latex) • Matt polyurethane varnish

TOOLS AND EQUIPMENT
Two 5 or 10cm (2 or 4in) paintbrushes • 2.5cm (1in) bristle paintbrush • Plasterboard (optional) • Soft pencil • Steel rule • Spirit level • 50 × 12mm (2 × ½in) wood batten – 60cm (24in) long • Two 5cm (2in) long wood blocks – cut from 4 × 4cm (1½ × 1½in) timber • Artist's nylon liner brushes (size 3 to 8 depending on thickness of line required) • Nylon watercolour brush (size 8 or smaller) • Cardboard • Scalpel • Old toothbrush

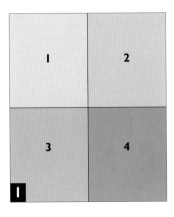

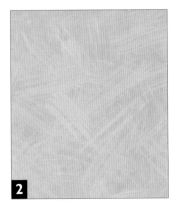

1 | Use a large brush to paint from ceiling to floor with one coat of white matt vinyl, with a touch of raw umber to 'knock down' the white. Choose or mix four shades of grey matt vinyl and paint two coats of the palest colour (no. 1) over the entire wall surface above the dado. Paint two coats of the second palest colour (no. 2) below the dado. Now, with the 2.5cm (1in) brush, paint a very soft, dragged effect up to and including the top of the dado rail using the darkest colour (no. 4). Stroke on the paint very lightly in horizontal sweeps for as long as the paint will last on the brush. Don't overload the brush as the paint must drag along the surface letting the base colour 'grin' through.

2 On a piece of plasterboard or another wall (already painted with the palest grey), practise the paint effect required above the dado. Using the second darkest colour (no. 3) and a 5cm (2in) brush (or a 10cm [4in] one if you want really large strokes), paint with the brushstrokes going in all different directions – horizontally, vertically and diagonally – so as to achieve an uneven finish, with the base colour, again, 'grinning' through. Work quickly across the wall, area by area, keeping the working edge wet. Once you are confident of the technique, you can start to work on the actual wall.

3 Decide upon the proportions and placing of the panels to suit the room and mark the panel lines lightly onto the wall with pencil, using a steel rule and a spirit level for accuracy. Make the lines thick and thin to create an impression of shadows on the moulding (see opposite).

Make a painting 'ruler' by nailing the two wood blocks to either end of the length of batten; use this to guide the painting of the moulding lines without risk of bleeding. Practise on some plasterboard or the spare wall: mix a little Prussian blue and a tiny touch of black artist's acrylic with colour no. 1, and

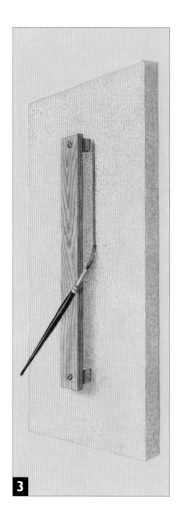

3

4

4 Cut a cardboard stencil of the stems using a scalpel, and use it to pencil their outlines lightly onto the wall, spacing them at consistent intervals. The design can be reversed, of course, for the top and bottom of the panel.

Mix a little burnt sienna artist's acrylic with colour no. 1 to make pale pink, adding a touch of white acrylic if necessary. Now paint in the stems with a nylon watercolour brush (again, you might chose to practise this technique). Load the brush with paint, and start very lightly, putting a little pressure on the brush towards the middle of the stem to widen the stroke, then wisping it up off the surface at the end of the stem. For an aged effect dab the stems with a natural sponge carrying a very little of colour no. 3; don't be afraid if this partially covers some of the stems. Paint each leaf in a single, flowing brushstroke, again pressing

use a lining brush to paint the lines. The distance of the batten from the surface may result in slightly wobbly lines, but this is preferable to their being dead straight. Once you are confident, start to work on the actual wall.

down in the middle and wisping off at the end.

Now age the entire wall above the dado by flicking a fine spray of paint no. 3 from an old toothbrush or cut down bristle brush (run your fingers along it and let the

bristles spring back). This gives a robin's egg effect.

If necessary, protect the area below the dado rail (including the skirting), together with the rail itself, by painting it with a coat of flat matt varnish.

FURNITURE

The furniture that characterizes Swedish interior design is quite diverse; it varies in style from eighteenth-century French rococo, through rustic country furniture to the eclecticism of the pieces in Carl Larsson's house. All the furniture in his turn-of-the-century parlour, dating from different periods, has a coherent and chic look because the overall colour scheme throughout the room is off-white, and the fact that the sofa and chairs have matching blue-and-white slip covers helps to pull the look together.

Larsson's paintings of his house provided the original inspiration for my interior designs, largely because his taste seemed so simple and so right for today. Ten years ago I thought I would be able to buy furniture like Larsson's in Sweden, but at that time nobody was making it, so I decided to design my own range of furniture. This was also influenced by the rustic pieces I had seen at Skansen Museum. When I design, I try to look back to the sources that might have inspired the original designer (such as French Provençal furniture) whilst keeping the essence of the Swedish piece, and maintaining this aspect throughout the range.

Most Swedish furniture is made in pine and then painted. In formal, sophisticated rooms it tends to be painted in off-whites, putty colours and pale French greys, and carries a natural sheen as if from years of use. This patina can be reproduced without much difficulty: for instance, a French reproduction Louis XVI chair 'in

'Introduce furniture sparingly, placing each piece with the whole room in mind.'

Opposite: Painted a pale muted green, this country-style chest of drawers combines French and Swedish design elements. On a pale khaki-and-cream diamond-patterned floor, which could be used in a sitting room or kitchen, it demonstrates how versatile this piece of furniture is. The formality of the panelled walls combines well, however, with the modest rustic feel of the chest of drawers. The arrangement here is a good example of simple symmetry.

Right: The design of this chair was inspired by a Carl Larsson illustration; it can either have a drop-in seat (as here) or a separate cushion (see page 72). My design for the small table, meanwhile, was influenced by a Swedish Biedermeier piece, though painted off-white like this, it takes on a completely different quality.

Above: The delicate, moulded ornamentation on this table was originally inspired by a Swedish sofa, although I have since seen the same decorative embellishment on a cabinet in England. I picked out the detailing in a very quiet pale blue on the palest of pale greys to avoid it being over-fussy.

the white' (which means the bare wood) can easily be given a painted, antiqued finish (see page 93). When I want to pick out a detail in a particular colour, especially on a delicately proportioned piece, I find it best to be as restrained as possible, and use a very pale blue, for instance, on an almost-white grey.

A piece of country furniture, meanwhile – a chest of drawers, for instance – can look wonderful in a stronger colour, mid-blue or green perhaps, but it should retain something of the muted feel. And I would recommend painting only one or two pieces in these stronger colours, keeping the rest of the room pale and calm.

ANTIQUING A TABLE

Antiquing wax enables you to reproduce the patina of antique French and Swedish painted furniture, with its natural sheen from years of wear. It is a wax to which colours have been added.

Of the few shades on the market, those closest in colour to raw umber are generally the most effective. The wax 'knocks down' the painted base colour, making it darker, as if with age, so it is important to test the combinations of base colour and wax before you start. Use matt vinyl rather than vinyl silk or eggshell as base coats of paint because the wax won't adhere to a shiny surface. Once the wax is absorbed it hardens to a satisfactorily strong finish for furniture, though it is not recommended for dining tables because the inevitable knocks, heat and spills can spoil the finish.

YOU WILL NEED:
MATERIALS
Table • Matt vinyl base colour
•Antiquing wax

TOOLS AND EQUIPMENT
4-5 cm (1½-2in) paintbrush •
Lint-free cotton rags •
Turpentine • Soft shoebrush

| Clean your table, fill holes and sand down.

2 Paint the table with three coats of matt vinyl, allowing it to dry and sanding down between coats.

3 Load your rag with wax and apply to legs and base. Wipe off any excess but not too much for a soft, dragged finish. If unhappy, remove with turps and start again.

4 Reload the rag and wipe the table top in straight parallel sweeps. Gently wipe off excess, leave for 15 minutes, then polish.

Both the table and chair here take antiquing wax very well, because all the decorative relief work collects more wax, helping to achieve a naturally aged look.

ACKNOWLEDGEMENTS AND SUPPLIERS

The author and publisher would like to thank the following for supplying or lending materials free of charge: Winther Browne, Manuel Canovas, Cologne and Cotton, The Dining Room Shop, The Blue Door, Chelsea Textiles, Judy Greenwood Antiques, Lunn Antiques, Nordic Style at Moussie, A Sanderson and Son, Anna Thomas, WH Newson, Wey Plastics, Nobilis-Fontan, Claridge and Co., Vaughan.

The author would like to thank the following for all their support and help: Sarah Baxter, Craig Cockfield, Charles Codrington, Suzanne Dennison, David Fitzpatrick, Henry Greenfield, Jim Haddon, Chris Heron, Katie O'Connor, Rachel Reynard, Kristina Saunders, Mr and Mrs Taylor-Davies, Clare Teed, Gavin Waddell, Jane Walker

Sasha Waddell Swedish Country Classics are distributed through: Kingshill Designs, Kitchener Works Kitchener Road, High Wycombe Bucks HP11 2SJ. 01494 463910

SUPPLIERS

Akzo Nobel Decorative Coatings
Lancashire 01254 704951
Crown Paints in matt, vinyl, eggshell, and other standard finishes

Anna Thomas
Middlesex 0181 892 0585
Swedish fabrics

Bell House and Co
London 0171 221 0187
Stocks Sasha Waddell furniture
Mail order available

The Blue Door
London 0181 748 9785
Swedish furniture and fabrics

Chelsea Textiles
London 0171 584 0111
Embroidered fabrics, bedspreads, pillow cases and checked fabrics

Claridge and Co.
London 0171 384 1265
Quilts

Cologne and Cotton
Warwickshire 01926 332573
New bedlinen

The Dining Room Shop
London 0181 878 1020
Furniture and china

Farrow and Ball Ltd
Dorset 01202 876141
Standard paint finishes

Fired Earth
Oxon 01295 812088
Delft tiles and natural flooring.
Mail order available

Henry Newbery
London 0171 636 2053
Trimmings, bobbles (wholesale)

Ian Mankin
London 0171 722 0997
Natural fabrics

Ikea
Croydon 0181 208 5600
Swedish furniture and fabrics

Isis Ceramics
Oxford 01865 722729
New blue-and-white china

Jali
Kent 01227 831710
Stocks Sasha Waddell radiator covers. Mail order available

John Myland Ltd.
London 0181 670 9161
Mylands Wax, antiquing wax

Judy Greenwood Antiques
London 0171 736 6037
Mirrors, beds, bedspreads, lighting, furniture; mostly antique French

Libra Antiques
London 0171 727 2990
Antique blue-and-white china

Lunn Antiques
London 0171 736 4638
Antique and new bedlinen

Manuel Canovas
London 0171 225 2298
French fabrics

The Malabar Cotton Co.
London 0171 978 5848
Natural fabrics

Nobilis-Fontan
London 0171 351 7878
French fabrics

Nordic Style at Moussie
London 0171 581 8674
Swedish furniture and fabrics
Stocks Sasha Waddell furniture

On the Tiles
London 0171 385 5480
Mexican tiles

Papers and Paints
London 0171 352 8626
Standard paint finishes. Ready-mixed raw umber and wetting agents

Pecheron
London 0171 580 5156
French fabrics

Pierre Frey
London 0171 376 5599
French fabrics

Robin Archer and Emma Temple
London 0181 960 1923
Specialist painters

Roger Oates
Herefordshire 01531 631611
Natural flooring and rugs

Sage Interiors
Surrey 01483 2244396
Stocks Sasha Waddell furniture

Sandersons
London 0171 584 3344
Stocks Sasha Waddell furniture
Mail order available

Soft Options
Cambridge 01223 311656
Swedish furniture and fabrics

Vaughan
London 0171 731 3133
Decorative lighting

Wey Plastics
London 0181 874 2003
MDF sheets of tongue-and-groove

W H Newson
London 0171 978 5000
Timber mouldings

Winther Browne
London 0181 803 3434
Decorative wood carvings

AUSTRALIA
Freedom Furniture
New South Wales (02) 436 3466
Swedish furniture and fabrics

Ikea
Victoria (03) 9555 5222
Swedish furniture and fabrics

NEW ZEALAND
Danske Moebler Furniture
Auckland (09) 625 3900
Furniture and fabrics

Levene & Co.
Auckland (09) 2744211
Paint and wallpaper

CANADA
Ikea
Vancouver (604) 273 2051
Swedish furniture and fabrics

Ikea
Montreal (514) 738 2167
Swedish furniture and fabrics

SOUTH AFRICA
Wunders Furniture
Cape Town (021) 47 5233
Furniture

The publisher thanks the
following photographers and
organizations for their
permission to reproduce the
photographs in this book:

7 **Andreas von Einsiedel**
House and Garden, The
Condé Nast Publications
9 –10 **David George**
Elizabeth Whiting
and Associates
11 above **Peo Eriksson**
11 below **Paul Ryan**
International Interiors
13 **Peo Eriksson**
14 **James Wedge**
16 **Ingalill Snitt**
17 left **Kari Haavisto**
18 **Paul Ryan**
International Interiors
22 **Peo Eriksson**
23 above **David George**
Elizabeth Whiting
and Associates
23 below **Peo Eriksson**
50 above **David George**
Elizabeth Whiting
and Associates
50 below **Paul Ryan**
International Interiors
51 **Peo Eriksson**
64 above **Peo Eriksson**
64 below **David George**
Elizabeth Whiting
and Associates
65 **David George**
Elizabeth Whiting
and Associates
66 **Gavin Kingcombe**
67 **Gavin Kingcombe**
77 **Ingalill Snitt**